The Perfect Match

Finding the ONE you were made for

WES RALEY

ISBN: 1987525310

ISBN-13: 9781987525311

10 9 8 7 6 5 4 3 2 1

Author's Note

This book was written for the people who at their worst moments have asked the question, "Is there anyone out there for me?" and at their best and most honest moments have admitted that deep down, they hope there is.

This is for people who have spent countless nights alone, wondering if this is how they are to live out the remainder of their days.

This is for the people who are dating or engaged to someone they are not made for but have hung on because they cannot bear the pain of being alone.

This book was written for *you.*

I know what it's like. I know the feeling of wondering if you will be alone forever or if marrying the person you are dating would be settling.

I know the feeling of wondering if you missed the right person or if there's even a "right" person to begin with.

I believe that I have a wealth of wisdom when it comes to finding the person that God wants you to be with because I have been in your shoes.

After going through a painful breakup with a woman I dated for over three years, I know how hard it can be to find the right one. I know what it's like to wonder if you are waiting in vain.

As hard as it was, the waiting I experienced prepared me for the day when I finally met my perfect match.

I have counseled many who feared lifelong singleness but eventually found *their* match as they patiently waited on God and trusted His timing. Through it all, I have found God's Word to be completely relevant to relationships.

In addition to my own story of finding my match, I have witnessed those who previously were heartbroken *find joy* as they patiently waited for the person God had for them.

There is nothing quite like watching someone find their perfect match.

May the practical wisdom in this book help you embrace the destiny God has for you and prepare you for a beautiful life with the person you were made for.

Dedication

This book is dedicated to the men who counseled, influenced, and helped me find my perfect match: Luke DeLisio, Barry Delks, and Jason Missi. You will never know how much your friendship, love, and support meant to me then and still do today. God sent you at just the right time, and I am eternally grateful for the role you played in guiding me to my match.

And to Korie, my amazing wife, of whom I can truly say, "Bone of my bones and flesh of my flesh!" We are the same, you and I—my very best friend and the love of my life. It is the honor of my life to be your husband.

Acknowledgements

A special thanks to the people who helped me refine and edit this book into the final product. I am so grateful for my book launch team including my beautiful wife Korie, Andy Bettencourt, Barry Delks, Chuck Herber, Josh Messmer, and Jim Taylor. You have given me wise feedback and provided much-needed encouragement along the way. Thank you for how you have loved me in this endeavor.

Foreword

Why should you read this book? Well, why does anyone read any book? Among other reasons, we read for entertainment, advice, instruction, information, inspiration, and correction. I believe you will encounter all of these in this volume.

You should read this book because of its author. I'd like to introduce you to my friend, Wes Raley. Wes is a compelling speaker; I have heard very few people who made me laugh more deeply and think more clearly than Wes does. He is a prophetic voice in his generation; he hears from God and communicates in a powerful way. He is not dry and didactic, nor is he preachy or confrontational; he writes in a conversational style—when I read the book, I felt more like Wes was in the room, speaking with me, encouraging me. He is passionate and enthusiastic, and it will be obvious on each page.

You should read this book because of its important subject matter. Dating relationships and marriage are some of the most critical pieces of our lives. They carry so much potential for our happiness and fulfillment, and they are fraught with so many dangers. This book can be of great help to you, whether you are single, single again, helping friends who are single, raising children who may marry one day, or merely wanting to grasp more firmly how God desires to work in our relationships. It contains wise advice, piercing observations, and godly counsel.

You should read this book because it can transform your life. Wes freely admits his own mistakes, so we won't have to repeat them. He presents some concepts that may be new to you, and you will have to wrestle with them. He gives specific examples of positioning yourself for God's blessing. He handles scripture reverently but forcefully. Some pages will comfort you, and others will make you uncomfortable; both are good for you. While reading the draft, I found myself repeatedly saying to my wife, "I wish we'd have known this before we married," and "I wish our children could have read this when they were dating."

I'm so thankful Wes and Korie have shared this part of their lives with us. They are examples of how God can use a couple when both are wholly devoted to Him. If you read this book all the way through, with an open mind and a teachable spirit, you will emerge with a greater confidence that God does indeed have a perfect match for *you*.

Dr. Jim Taylor Jr.
Mooresville, Indiana
June 2018

CityChangersIndiana.com

Table of Contents

Introduction:
It's True

What if, in the course of making you for a specific *purpose*, God also made you for a specific *person*?

What if the innate belief and hope you have felt deep in your soul that there was someone out there for you was actually put there by God Himself? What if it were true?

I have great news for you: *It is true.*

I'm not talking about the people God gifts with singleness, though it could be argued that even they are perfectly matched with fellowship, accountability, and love.

I am talking about the romantic—that's the person I was made for—kind of love.

So many people today live with the fear of being alone for the rest of their lives. They strongly desire the companionship that "true love" would offer them. But so many things seem to stand in the way.

Constantly seeing other couples share the joy of life together can bring a feeling of emptiness to your soul—but only when it's stripped from this reality: *God has not forgotten you.*

God is still in the business of making perfect matches today.

Some are settling for relationships (everything from casually dating to engaged) which are not God's *best* for them, but they are frightened to leave that person in exchange for the possibility of no one at all.

I know all of these feelings and more because I lived with the fear of being alone for many years. I stayed in a relationship for over three years because fear had a stranglehold over my life.

But thankfully, the God who perfectly matches people together intervened in such a powerful way that I was able to end that relationship with integrity, having no one else to go to. This was because I believed with all my heart that God had a perfect match for me.

And He did.

But He doesn't force His plan on anyone. It takes someone who is willing to surrender their plans and timing to His perfect sovereignty—to allow His peace to shatter their fears and lead them into their destiny.

We see all throughout the Bible that God is acutely aware of our personal pains and our deepest desires. He longs to be gracious to us and lead us into His plan for our lives.

My life was forever changed when I started to believe that God's plan for my life *included* leading me to my perfect match.

When God made Eve out of Adam's rib, it led Adam to exclaim, *"This **at last** is bone of my bones and flesh of my flesh!"* (Genesis 2:23, ESV). This Hebrew idiom incorporates the emotion of Adam's longing and the power of God's fulfillment. "I *finally* found my match!"

In the same way, God continues His work today of sovereignly orchestrating the very matches He has designed.

So would you pause your fear, disbelief, and the pain of the past long enough to consider what the scriptures teach on this subject?

This book isn't about finding a perfect person—because you can't! It is about finding *your* match. It's only perfect because of the One who designed it to begin with. God's work is never lacking, and He takes great care to design and fit the pieces of His plan together in harmony.

The best part is, God redeems all the pieces of our messy past and the growing pains of our future to paint a picture worth seeing, a masterpiece worth beholding, and a relationship that is as intricate as it is incredible. *He wastes nothing.*

I hope you'll join me in this adventure on the road to your perfect match—the path which is carved out by God's sovereignty and traversed by trusting in Him.

After all, we trust Him to be our Strength, our Shield, our Hope, our Refuge, our Fortress, our Provider, our Physician, and our Maker—why not trust Him to be the *Perfect Matchmaker?*

Part I: The Promise

01

Tears Before Joy

Tears Of Pain

*Those who sow with **tears will reap** with songs of joy. Those who go out weeping, carrying seed to sow, will return with songs of joy, carrying sheaves with them.* **Psalm 126:5-6**

I remember turning toward the wall one night while laying in bed at my parents' house during college and praying a prayer that would radically change the rest of my life.

I'm not sure of the exact words I used, but I know that something finally broke inside of me. I finally agreed with God in what I believe He had been trying to show me for so long: He *did* have someone out there for me.

I faced the wall and prayed with urgency because I knew that I couldn't stay on the fence for much longer—I needed God to get me out of the relationship I had gotten myself into.

As I laid in my bed, I had to wrestle with the question which had plagued me for some time now: *Does God have someone with whom I am supposed to spend the rest of my life?*

God speaks to us in all sorts of ways. But that night, I didn't hear a message as much as I felt a *major shift* occur in my heart.

The sudden shift I felt in that moment was because I surrendered. In a moment's time, I finally accepted the reality that the woman I was dating was not the person I was made for.

I felt peace rush in as I rested in God's sovereignty. But that was quickly chased out by the thought of what I had to do next.

Perseverance Precedes Your Destiny

It was the hardest decision I've ever had to make. It was also the most fruitful, blessed, and life-giving. But the fruit followed the hard choice, and it didn't come as quickly as I would have preferred.

Through breaking up with the woman I had dated for over three years, I learned that those who sow in tears reap with songs of joy. It's interesting to me that those two things often go hand-in-hand, tears and joy.

Painful situations and decisions often bear the most fruit in our lives. Perhaps it's the character that's built through hardships, waiting, and distress. Or maybe it's something even deeper. *It's almost as if it's a spiritual reality that our destinies lie on the other side of perseverance.*

When I broke up with Ashley (not her real name), my whole world felt like it was in a tailspin. But at the same time, beneath all of the pain, I finally had hope rekindling in my heart. I felt a deep-rooted conviction inside of me like I had never felt before. It was like a tangible certainty deep in the core of my being—I knew that God had a match out there for me.

I felt joy at the thought that I was done with doing it my own way and was ready to submit to God's plan for my life. But let me back up just a bit.

From Single To Steady

Coming out of a public high school and entering college with no girlfriend was not an easy transition to make. Most of my friends moved away, and while I never seriously dated anyone in high school, I was the exception among my friend group.

Most of my friends were either in a relationship that *looked like* it was headed toward marriage (many times it wasn't) or were constantly jumping from person to person in what seemed like a never-ending search to make them happy.

I'll admit, my tendency was to fall into the latter group. I wouldn't find out until years later that I was nursing an insecurity inside of myself which I pacified by always dating someone.

Somehow, I had embraced a belief that *who I was with determined how much I was worth*. When I wasn't dating someone, I was always looking for someone to date.

Insecurity was my filter.

I had a few short-lived relationships in high school, but it wasn't until college that I found myself in my first serious relationship. We broke up nine months later when I found out she was unfaithful from the beginning of our relationship.

This betrayal was like pouring gasoline on a fire that was already consuming my peace. It only further compounded the issue I struggled with of needing to have a significant other in order to feel valuable.

My worth was wrapped up in another person, not God.

After having a dream where I forgave this girl and waking up to a tremendous feeling of peace, God led me to forgive her early on. God knew that adding unforgiveness to my loneliness would've only led me to a deeper valley.

So I was able to move on, but I went right back to trying to fill the void in my soul.

Masking The Void

From the pain of that rejection, and without much time to recover, I did what I always did—started looking for someone else. That is when I met Ashley.

I didn't seek God's will or wait on His timing to show me that I was ready to move on. Instead, I did one of the craziest things I have ever done.

After dropping her off from one of our first dates, I remember coming home to my parents' house and getting down on my knees in the living room to say a prayer. I'll never forget what I prayed: "God I ask that you would bless my efforts here and that *even if it's not your will* you would let her date me."

I cannot tell you how *strongly* I recommend not praying that prayer. It was clear that my insecurity was driving my actions to a place of insanity. I mean, come on—I was basically doing the opposite of Jesus' "Thy will be done" prayer and saying, "God, I think my plan is better!" Over three years later, I realized how foolish that prayer was.

I'm not saying God gave me what I wished for. I really don't know how all that works. But I do believe that God gives us free will. He never forces His will on anyone, and since I was content to try and *force* my own way, then *my own way* is exactly what I got.

<u>Breaking Up</u>

The turning point for me in finding the perfect match was not when I eventually met my future wife Korie but when I made the hardest decision of my life to end my relationship with Ashley.

It required a trust in God like I had never walked in before. In the months to follow, I felt a new depth to my relationship with the LORD as He taught me to trust in *His* ability to bring about *His* plans for my life.

It's on that note that I would like to address many of you who have been broken up with by a significant other. While I was the one that chose to end this relationship, I have been broken up with in the past. The pain of rejection by someone you care about is something that only those who have walked through it can identify with. The feeling of unworthiness that can manifest when another person says they don't want to be with you is something you wouldn't wish on your worst enemy.

That being said, if you have been broken up with or divorced by your spouse, the call in this book to trust in God's sovereignty is all the more tangible for you. Can you trust that God has your best in mind and will turn this around for your good?

Please take it from someone who has been rejected in the past—God will heal your pain and redeem what you've been through in ways you could never imagine!

If you were the one who was rejected, you can rest in God's sovereignty knowing that it was out of *your* control—but totally within *His*. Trying to stay in a dating relationship with someone who feels led to move on from you would only be manipulation, a heart attitude which is unable to receive God's best for our lives.

Hard Times

When I finally surrendered to God's leading, I had to make the hard decision to break up with Ashley. It was something that I agonized about for a long time. What was so hard about it? Here were my five biggest obstacles:

1) It hurt her deeply.

I hated the idea that I was causing someone pain largely because of my own issues over the years like complacency and the fear of being alone. Not only that—it hurt the people close to us who had invested in our relationship. Friends and family of hers who saw how hurt she was were also disappointed in me. They wondered what the catalyst was because on the surface everything appeared to be fine.

2) The fear of making the wrong decision was paralyzing.

Without God gracefully showing me that I was supposed to move on, I would've probably stayed forever. He didn't put a note under my pillow or write a message on my wall (I would've welcomed those things!). But He *did* give me continued confirmations through His Word, prayer, my experiences, and the counsel of my faith community who also helped me reach that conclusion.

By the way, I never told her that I believed God had someone else for me or anything like that. I will talk about how to honor the person you are breaking up with in a later chapter, but for now, please know that I did not try to push everything off on God or say, "God told me to break up with you." What I did share with Ashley was that we were on different wavelengths and had two different worldviews.

I was afraid that if I broke up with Ashley and never found someone else, I would regret it for the rest of my life. What if she found someone else but then I realized I was wrong?

That fear kept me trapped in the relationship for far too long.

Fear never propels us to God's path—it detours us from being the person He has called us to be.

Fear is an enemy to your destiny.

3) I was afraid of being alone.

This showed that I was not comfortable to be with myself, wasn't satisfied with God, and was finding my fulfillment in other people. That is called co-dependency.

My worth was wrapped up in her and not in God. He showed me that I needed to trust Him and end things without having someone else to go to. I wanted to end things with integrity, but I knew that would mean a period of singleness and healing.

4) After investing so much time in that relationship, I felt like I would be wasting it all to cut things off now.

At that point, I had invested about 15% of my life with Ashley. She was the closest person in my life at the time. She knew the most about me. We saw each other almost every single day, and we had several mutual friends. Also, both of us had become close to each other's parents. All of that is to say, it felt like starting over again would be nullifying over three years of my life. In the grand scheme of things, we were probably just six months or so away from getting engaged, which would have solidified things even further.

5) Somewhere along the way, I had embraced a theology that God wanted me to stick with it no matter how hard it was or how much I didn't line up with someone.

I have received a lot of bad teaching over the years that it is prideful to not stick with something or that humility always chooses to stay. I don't believe that anymore!

While it will always be true that growing together in relationships *requires a commitment* to one another, when it comes to dating, it is also true that sometimes you can *grow apart*. Another way of saying it would be that it is no longer healthy for you to stay in the relationship. This is why it is so important that you seek God's discernment and surround yourself with a faith community to walk alongside of you in these matters.

It is not humility to stay with someone who is not your match!

It may be easier in the short term, but later is a whole lot more important than the ease of "now."

By the way, I'm not talking about marriage here, and I'll explain why in Chapter 3. But suffice it to say, dating and engagement are the time for deciding if you will commit to this relationship for life.

"Failure" Can Be God's Grace

We cannot be afraid of failure! I think that some people stay in a dating relationship simply because pride prevents them from the appearance of failure.

I personally believe it is not a failure to find out that someone isn't your match. You continue to grow in discernment about how, when, and who to enter a relationship with. It's not a failure at all!

It was God's grace for this relationship to come to an end. Let's just say that if God had not carried me, I would not have had the courage to do what I knew needed to be done.

I used to pray, "God please just open the door, and I will walk through it." The hard moments have taught me that the truer reality is, "God, please open the door *and carry me through it!*"

I am so thankful that we have a God who is willing to do just that! He not only guides us, but as we let go and trust Him, He carries us.

Let The Tears Flow

Without giving all of the details, it was a painful breakup. When I went to break up with Ashley, I couldn't bring myself to say the words. Even though she didn't want me to end things, she graciously told me to just tell her what she knew I had to say. So as painful as it was, I did.

After the breakup was official, I ran to the next people closest to me, my parents. I wanted them to tell me that I had made the right decision and that I didn't need to be afraid of being alone forever. While I didn't get that certainty from them, the Person I truly needed to entrust my future to was God.

He was the One who held my destiny securely in His hands. I knew I had to stay faithful to what I believed He was promising me—that there was a perfect match for me.

I learned that sometimes when we make life-altering decisions, we grow the most by genuinely walking with God step-by-step, not by being instructed by others for every decision.

This creates true dependence on the LORD and helps us make decisions that we can maintain when the opinion of the crowd changes.

Learning to hear from God is a critical part of walking in His will. The good news is, God wants to speak to all of us!

*I will instruct you and teach you in the way you should go; I will counsel you with my loving eye on you. **Do not be like the horse** or the mule, which have no understanding but **must be controlled** by bit and bridle or they will not come to you.*
Psalm 32:8-9

This is God's way of reminding us that our need and dependency should be on Him. When we look to God for direction in this way, we won't be needy toward others or controlled by them.

That being said, I am so grateful for the way my mother comforted and counseled me in this difficult time. She came to my room where I was bawling my eyes out and asked if she could pray with me.

We got down on our knees together and I prayed and asked God one request—that on my wedding day someday in the unknown future, my mom and I could get down on our knees again and thank God for the pain that I was currently experiencing. That thought gave purpose to my pain.

It was a prophetic moment that gave me hope and a conviction that I *had* to go through *this* to get to the *one* I was made for. It was an act of faith—acknowledging God's goodness and plans for me in the midst of this pain.

It gave me a vision to hold on to of my future wedding day where all of this pain would be worth it.

At the beginning of this chapter, I shared a verse about how our tears actually pave the way for a future harvest. Something inside of me desired to walk in faith with that reality. So after my Mom left my room that day, I got down and picked up my tissues—wet with all my tears—and put them in a ziplock bag. I imagined that one day, I would get them out and be able to hold in my hands both *the proof of the pain* and *the reward of the wait*.

Healing Through Hurting

Painful days followed as I learned how to navigate what *actually* breaking up with someone looked like.

One of those days was when Ashley called to say that she had boxed up all of the gifts from me or objects that reminded her of our relationship and asked if she could give them back. They were too painful to keep. I told her that would be fine.

The next day, one of her friends drove her to my house, and she left them on my front porch. I'll admit, seeing some of the mementos made me sad for the death of what was once precious to me. But the conviction of what God was calling me to and the belief that there was a perfect match out there for me kept me strong when nostalgia threatened to steal my destiny.

A couple of days after she dropped the items off, she had a change of heart and asked that I bring them back to her. So this time with my friend Luke in tow, I dropped off the box at her house for what would be the last face-to-face conversation we ever had.

She asked if I would carry the box inside for her, and I obliged. Taking a last look around the house that had become so familiar to me was a somber moment to endure. I gave her greyhound dog one last pat on the head and turned to leave, saying goodbye to Ashley for the final time. Her cries as I left for good were almost too much to bear, and as I headed back to my truck where Luke was waiting, I let the tears flow.

As we pulled away from her house, my tears turned to sobs. I don't think Luke knew what to do, so he just stayed silent.

Eventually, I was able to muster these words which were etched in my brain when I would later look for a wife: "I never want to hurt someone like that again. I truly want the next person I date to be the person that I marry. With all of my heart, I want to wait for God's perfect match."

And that's exactly what happened.

02

The Theology of the Perfect Match

Don't Give Up

Let me speak directly to those of you reading this book who have given up on the idea that God has someone out there for you. I understand how frustrating it can be if you are single or even in a mediocre relationship to hear about the joys of finding the perfect match. But please, whatever you do, don't give up.

In the Kingdom of God, surrender isn't giving up, *it's letting go.*

I invite you to discover with me the freedom of trusting God to orchestrate your destiny and to enjoy your journey along the way.

Before we get into the theology of what I believe will be a game-changer for countless singles, this fact must be front-and-center: *You can trust God with your destiny.*

When I say "destiny," I'm referring to God's plan for your life. His sovereignty is beyond our comprehension. But as you will see through scripture, God never violates our free will. I use the word destiny because His sovereignty is much bigger than our ability to figure it all out.

I realize that I do not understand your particular situation or how long it's been or how frustrated you may have become.

I remember how frustrated I would get when married people would tell me that God had a match for me and to wait for His perfect timing. That was easy for *them* to say! But when I finally saw what *God* said, I had an entirely different perspective.

As I reflected on my multiple failed relationships, I began to realize that I had pursued them according to my own thoughts and desires and had never really considered what *God* had to say about finding His very best for me.

At that point, I decided that if there was any wisdom to be found about relationships, surely the Bible must have it. And that's where I made some of the most profound discoveries about finding my perfect match.

But before I share those, I want to explain to you what I mean by a "perfect" match.

Perfect?

This book isn't about finding a perfect *person* or even a perfect *relationship*—because there aren't any! Looking for the perfect *person* will keep you trapped in the lonely discontentment of impossible expectations.

This book is about finding *your* perfect match. Meaning the person that God has made to fit *you*.

It is only perfect because of the One who designed it to begin with. God's work is never lacking or incomplete.

> *Every **good and perfect gift** is from above, coming down from the Father of the heavenly lights, who does not change like shifting shadows.* **James 1:17**

I am merely choosing to use the language that God uses throughout His Word to describe His gifts to us. The Bible says that His gifts are never bad or imperfect. They are "good and perfect." The word "perfect" is simply a reflection of His nature!

Does perfect mean it will be easy? No way! As human beings in this world, we still mess up. We change. We grow. But through it all, God remains constant, and His gifts remain perfect.

If you remember, Adam and Eve still messed up and had some pretty major relationship issues for a time. But could you ever in a million years say that they were *not* God's perfect match? Could you ever say that they were *not* made for each other? Absolutely not—because perfect matches aren't perfect due to *performance* but due to God's *sovereignty*—they are *His* idea, *His* plan, and *His* gift to us.

God Is A Matchmaker

From the very beginning of the Bible, I believe God not only shows us that He *does* make perfect matches, but He also shows how we are supposed to operate since this is true.

The theology of this book goes all the way back to the very first human relationship—Adam and Eve. Has it ever crossed your mind that God was the first Matchmaker in history?

When everything was as it should be, before sin ever entered the world, before there was ever a problem to troubleshoot, a need for counseling, or a teaching on conflict resolution—*God took the initiative* to make the perfect match.

In the first chapter of Genesis, we see God creating things one day at a time. Then, at the end of each day, He seems to pause and evaluate the work that He had accomplished.

*And God saw that **it was good.** Genesis 1:10*

God did this over and over again. He created things all day long, and as He desired, He stepped back and evaluated His work. Plants, stars, fish, birds, animals. Good. Good. Good. Good. Good. Everything He made was called "good" or "tohv"[1] in the Hebrew, with two exceptions.

The first exception to being called "good" was us!

On the sixth day, He created man. At the end of that day, He didn't say it was simply "tohv," He said that it was "tohv meode"[2] or "*very* good" (Genesis 1:31).

He went one step further to call us *very* good. This shows that God holds us as the apple of His eye—the pinnacle of His creation.

The reason why this is important for our discussion on relationships is the stark contrast between this and the second exception for "good."

> *The Lord God said, "It is **not good** for the man to be alone. I will make a helper suitable for him."* **Genesis 2:18**

*The second exception f*or everything being called good was when God called something "*not* good."

It was *not good* for man to be alone.

Think about that! *Everything* God made was at least good. And humans were actually called "*very* good." But the one thing that we see—and this was before sin entered the world —that was inherently not good was "for the man to be alone."

Now, the idea that there could be something "not good" in the midst of God's perfect creation raises a whole host of theological questions for me. But for the sake of staying on topic, I want to simplify things a bit.

Let's look at the problem of man being alone (which is still a problem today) and God's solution to the problem (which is still the solution today).

How It Was Meant To Be

Here are seven things we see going on with God's first ever perfect match:

1) From God's perspective (and He's always right), it's not a good thing to be alone.

> *The Lord God said, "It is **not good** for the man **to be alone.** I will make a helper suitable for him."* **Genesis 2:18**

Our culture in America is often one of independence in an adverse way. We like to "go our own way" and "do it alone." We say things like, "I don't need anybody!" Or, "I can take care of myself!"

But since God made us in His image, we were designed for community. The Trinity is a complex yet perfect example of the interconnectedness of relationships that we are supposed to experience.

We were created in the image of a God who is most appropriately represented by *relationship*: Father, Son, and Holy Spirit.

So we need to realize from the start that it is by God's design that we would not be alone for the rest of our lives.

Remember, this was not like Adam did something which *caused* "being alone" to be "not good." No, being alone was not good from the beginning of time! In other words, we are made for relationships *by design.*

The Gift Of Singleness

I will briefly mention the gift of singleness here and cover it more thoroughly in the next chapter. The gift of singleness frightens many single people, but it doesn't need to.

It's clear that if God gives the gift of singleness, it will be exactly that—a *gift.* No one should ever fear that God is going to *punish* them with singleness since He is incapable of giving bad gifts!

And by its very definition, the gift of singleness can't be the same thing as being alone because that would mean God is giving a gift that is "not good."

My point is that by design we are not supposed to be alone. We were designed for the perfect match.

Even with the gift of singleness, God still gives perfect matches of fellowship, accountability, and love. And ultimately, as we will explore later, *Jesus is forever our Perfect Match.*

In this book, we will primarily be talking about how God has a perfect match in terms of a spouse for us, just as we see in this Genesis account of creation.

2) God alone is the Perfect Matchmaker.

> *The Lord God said, "It is not good for the man to be alone.* **I will make** *a helper suitable for him."* **Genesis 2:18**

God is the only One who can make perfect matches. Do you see how clear this is? We will see it even clearer when He carries out what He is promising to Adam—and you will see it even clearer when God carries out what He is promising to you!

It is futile, even silly for you to try to make someone fit your life. It is equally futile to try to track down the right relationship. God's sovereignty must be the higher reality in this entire process, or you will live with the fear of missing out!

Can you trust God to bring about the very match that He has designed?

3) God makes people *for* one another (i.e. perfect matches).

> The Lord God said, "It is not good for the man to be alone. I will make a helper **suitable for him."**
> **Genesis 2:18**

Do you see it in the verse? God actually crafted Eve with Adam in mind.

As much as this truth may make some people uncomfortable, the indisputable fact is that God *at least* made one person *for* someone else. He *at least* had *one* perfect match in mind. And I'd like to propose to you that if God did it this way the *first time* for the *first couple* before anything ever went wrong, then this is the higher reality of relationships.

God is the Perfect Matchmaker, and He delights in designing each person with their match in mind.

God took Adam's bone and used it to make Eve! It was as if there was a part of him in her very makeup, her DNA, her design. And based on my take, God wasn't super worried about the fact that people might look at this first example and believe that the same could be true for them.

Please hold your disbelief, cautions, and exceptions until the next chapter. For now, could you bask in awe of the sovereignty of the God who not only wrote all of your days down in a book before you were born (Psalm 139:16) but also fashioned your DNA to be the right person for your future lover?

4) God never reveals a need without a desire to fill it.

> *Now the Lord God had formed out of the ground all the wild animals and all the birds in the sky. He brought them to the man to see what he would name them; and whatever the man called each living creature, that was its name.* ***So the man gave names** to all the livestock, the birds in the sky and all the wild animals. **But for Adam, no suitable helper was found.*** **Genesis 2:19-20**

Amazing—God had Adam go through all the animals only to realize there was no fit!

I wonder how long this took—all of this searching with no match to be found.

I wonder if in the waiting Adam grew doubtful after he made his way through every animal that wasn't his match.

I wonder how long God waited to bring about Adam's desire.

I wonder how long *you* have waited.

If you've been waiting a long time for your match, you should be encouraged here. I'm guessing the naming of all of the animals in the whole world took some time.

The truth is, we see that even the first human had to do his fair share of waiting for his match.

It seems like God was making Adam thirst for the right fit by showing him many wrong fits.

Could it be that God is the one making you thirst for the right relationship?

Sometimes we have to find out what we are *not* looking for before we know what we *are* looking for.

Your past was not without purpose! Perhaps all of the "failure" was God's way of showing you who you were *not* made for!

God *wanted* Adam to see his need—but not so that Adam would live in disappointment. God is not the God of disappointment!

God Is A Rewarder

> *But without faith it is impossible to please Him, for he who comes to God must believe that He is, and that **He is a rewarder** of those who diligently seek Him.* **Hebrews 11:6 NKJV**

God is a Rewarder! Many people believe that God is real, but so many see Him as a Punisher and not a Rewarder.

In short, people who think that God is punishing them by making them stay single are believing a lie because being alone is called "not good" by the Person who defines what good and bad are.

Whose Desires?

I would like to remind you that God *wants* to give you the desires of your heart.

*Take delight in the LORD, and He will give you **the desires of your heart**.* **Psalm 37:4**

This will be a pivotal verse for the entire book.

If I am taking God's Word for what it actually says, then I must point out that Psalm 37:4 says God will give you the desires of *your* heart.

Sadly, I have seen many people try to twist this verse to say that when we delight ourselves in God He will *change* our desires. But does it say that? No! It says that He will give us the desires of *our* hearts.

This doesn't mean that God *never* changes our desires—we know He does! But the exchange in this verse isn't talking about that at all.

I think that sometimes when we see unmet desires in ourselves or others, we are too quick to settle. We think that it must mean God wants something different.

As we have seen with Adam, God is often the one who *puts* our desires within us!

If I could only convince one thing to the many Christians I have interacted with over the years, it would be that God is *not* the God of disappointment!

It makes me sad that many religious-minded people think God only wants to *change* our desires when the reality is He longs to be gracious to us and *fulfill* our deepest desires.

Can people have unholy desires? Absolutely. It's important for us to surrender all to God—even our desires—and let Him determine our destiny. But just as we already talked about, surrendering our desires isn't giving up on them but letting them go to the One who knows best.

The truth is, many of us have embraced a false belief system where we think that everything we desire must be against God's will. This views God as a cruel Father!

A Generous Father

*If you, then, though you are evil, know how to give good gifts to your children, **how much more will your Father** in heaven give good gifts to those who ask Him!* **Matthew 7:11**

I want to encourage you to base your views of God on actual scripture. He is a good Father who knows how to give perfect gifts to His children!

God doesn't withhold things cruelly *from* us like a carrot on a string but *for* us like a present until Christmas.

He waits to give gifts at the right time.

I want my children to have everything good that they can as long as it doesn't hurt them. For example, I want my children to have money and be able to drive a car. My oldest child is only five years old, so giving these things early would be a cruel thing to do. He must mature first because they could harm him if not used properly.

In the same way, God waits to give gifts when they will be a blessing to us.

So don't assume that God's *delay* is His *denial*.

Just like Adam, God wants to fulfill the desires that He reveals in you.

God was acutely aware of Adam's desires—because He put them there! Sometimes, God leads us by showing us what we are truly thirsting for.

I'm saying, could it be that if you are longing for a spouse that it was God who put that longing there to begin with?

Has God revealed this to you like He did to Adam?

5) It is not on you to make it happen.

> So the Lord God caused the man to fall into a deep sleep; and **while he was sleeping,** He took one of the man's ribs and then closed up the place with flesh. Then the Lord God made a woman from the rib He had taken out of the man, and **He brought her to the man. Genesis 2:21-22**

"*He* brought her to the man."

Powerful!

In all of your searching, you could overlook this amazing truth: *It is God's job to bring together the very matches He has designed.*

Adam's role was to rest. He had to get to a place where he allowed God to have full control. The same is true for you. God is happy to put you into a deep sleep when you stop trying to do His job for Him.

Remember, all of Adam's searching for animals revealed who was *not* a perfect match.

It is easy to strive and strain thinking of every possible match —sizing up every new encounter, hoping, and even stretching in our minds how they could fit us. The truth is, God does His best work when we stop being backseat drivers.

Imagine the freedom you would feel if you decided to trust God so deeply that while you were going about the ordinary business of serving Him, He brought along the person you were made for.

Can you trust God to do it His way?

Hopefully you know that I am not telling you to lock yourself in your bedroom and ignore phone calls from potential suitors. The real question is, which side of the fence are you on?

Are you truly in danger of being so passive about finding the right person that you could miss them? Or are you more in danger of taking matters into your own hands?

It may be time for you to get out of the cockpit and back in the passenger seat. Sometimes God lets you yank the throttle out of His hands so that you will learn to appreciate relaxing in first class again.

6) God's perfect match for you will match.

> *The man said,*
> *"This is now **bone of my bones**
> **and flesh of my flesh;***
> *she shall be called 'woman,'*
> *for she was taken out of man."* **Genesis 2:23**

Opposites attract. Well, that's true unless they don't.

While it's true that God designs different personality traits to complement our matches (e.g. "he likes to talk and she loves to listen" or "she loves to joke and he loves to laugh"), the truth is we are designed to look at our spouse with a "she gets me" and "you were made for me" kind of love.

"Bone of my bones and flesh of my flesh" is a Hebrew idiom which implies "we match—we are the same!"

Again, I am not talking about having differences or personalities that complement each other. These things should be celebrated.

My wife complements and balances me out in so many ways, it's ridiculous! She is able to give me perspective and insight that I would've never thought of. So being different is not bad at all. I'm talking about the importance of having *unity* about the things that matter.

It is critical that you share the same values and belief systems.

There are so many examples I could give you. Someone who isn't an actual born-again Christian or who views social issues from a pagan perspective will only cause you sorrow later on. Or someone who is super critical while you are a grace-oriented person will make you want to sleep in separate bedrooms!

> *Better to live on a corner of the roof than share a house with a quarrelsome wife.* **Proverbs 25:24**

7) Shifting loyalties is a necessity for oneness.

> *That is why a man **leaves his father and mother** and is united to his wife, and they **become one** flesh. Adam and his wife were both naked, and they felt no shame.* **Genesis 2:24-25**

This really matters a lot when you find your match because your new relationship will alter the status of your previous relationships.

As you are waiting for God's perfect match, you should prepare your heart now for the reality that your parents and even best friends will not be your go-to sources of comfort and counsel for the rest of your life.

Couples who my wife and I counsel that struggle with conflict resolution usually have a "tell-all" person in their relationship. This most often is one of the parents, and based on experience, it's often their mothers.

My wife Korie and I write about this in our forthcoming book, *Forsaking All Others*—which is about how to have a marriage worth leaving all behind.

My point isn't that you need to grow distant or withdraw. Not at all! However, the reality that your loyalties will shift in the future should give you perspective about how to order your life now.

In fact, there is *so much* you can do right now to prepare!

In light of the future changes and shifts in loyalty that will take place once God brings your match, how should you be living right now? This requires faith!

Get Ready

Perhaps the length of time you have already waited has become your indicator or gauge as to what to expect in the future. Don't let it be! God is all-powerful. Don't order your life as if your match will never come along. Choosing today to walk in faith will be the best preparation for when God, as soon as He sees fit, will bring along your perfect match.

While we see from the Genesis account that it's God who brings along our perfect match in His way and His timing, there are *many* things you can be doing to prepare yourself for that amazing relationship.

Those things will be the focus for the remainder of this book.

03

Exceptions Aren't the Rule!

No Vision

The times when I have publicly shared the insights in this book were usually met with incredible gratitude from singles who were not used to such practical Biblical teaching about waiting for their match. It gave them a hope and a vision of what God had for them in the future. Some had given up on finding a match years ago and were begrudgingly resigned to "go it alone" the rest of their life. But when they heard the things you will read in this book, they were stirred to believe God for the fulfillment of their deepest desires. No longer did they try to pretend like they didn't mind, they came to God honestly and poured out their heart to Him—asking Him to help them believe and wait for His perfect match for them.

This really is the nature of prophetic ministry—it paints a picture of what God is up to, what He is promising, and what He will bring to pass. Many singles today are incredibly discouraged because they have no vision, and without a vision, people perish (Proverbs 29:18).

I believe that, sadly, one of the major reasons for discouragement among singles is due to the fact that many leaders are afraid to teach about these wonderful promises. In part, they refrain for fear that it will offend those who have been single for many years with no match in sight. But they are especially afraid that sharing these truths may be inadvertently promising things that are not true—not true for *everyone*, that is. And that's the problem, they are afraid to teach confidently about finding a perfect match for fear of the exceptions. So they determine their teaching by the few examples that seem to go against what I am saying. They exclude incredible testimonies from the many because of the fear of false interpretations of the few. They wonder, what if it doesn't come true for *everyone*? In my mind, that seems like trying to pad the results for God! Will we not fully trust Him to come through and do what He has promised?

This grieves my heart on many levels, but namely, when we refuse to share these amazing truths, we leave so many people stuck in fear, insecurity, frustration, and loneliness—all the while secretly holding the antidote!

Many of these life-changing messages from scripture are purposefully filtered by ministry leaders so that the watered-down version will neither offend anyone nor help them. I cannot tell you what I would've given to be taught the truths in this book earlier in life when I was single! Thankfully, God is not like those fearful leaders, and He is happy to guide us into *all* truth (John 16:13).

No One Can Fathom

> *Do you not know? Have you not heard? The LORD is the everlasting God, the Creator of the ends of the earth. He will not grow tired or weary, and His understanding **no one can fathom**.* **Isaiah 40:28**

I do not pretend to understand how all of this works. God's sovereignty is beyond our ability to fully comprehend it. No one can fathom His understanding! But thankfully, we don't have to *understand* everything to be able to *trust* Him. In fact, the Bible tells us to "Trust in the LORD with all your heart and lean not on your own understanding" (Proverbs 3:5). So the reality is, trusting God *cannot* be dependent on our ability to understand or figure things out.

My point is that I could never try to address every exception or extenuating circumstance in this book. This book was written to encourage single people who desire a spouse to trust the Perfect Matchmaker!

I may not understand every facet of God bringing about matches, but what I *do* understand is that when I started operating according to the belief that God *did have someone for me* and not just *something for me to do*, it was a game-changer in my life!

This belief only produced a healthy outlook about how to operate while I was single, and it gave me an incredible hope and vision for the future.

Oh, and by the way, it was *true*! God *did* have someone for me! I'm glad that I didn't listen to the cautious leaders and instead listened for God's confirmation of a spouse for me.

So my intention in this book is not to water down the reality of perfect matches, nor is it to promise every person a spouse. The LORD is God, let Him do as He sees fit (1 Samuel 3:18).

Pushback From The Leaders

Most people are excited for me and thankful that I share how God was so gracious to lead me out of the wrong relationship and later to the person He had for me. But some leaders would be happy for me to just tell my story and not suggest to others that God will do the same for them. But God is not a respecter of persons (Acts 10:34)!

I refuse to believe that what He did for me He wouldn't do for someone else. Of course, God doesn't have to do things the same way (and rarely does, it seems!). But in the core of my being, I believe that God wants me to share what He did in my life because of the hope it could give others that God would do it for them too!

It seems to me that many in the faith sector have become so afraid of being misunderstood or of God not coming through that they hesitate to share a life-changing message for fear of how it could be falsely interpreted!

It is like they are *protecting* God's image instead of *bearing* God's image.

We don't have to protect God's reputation! He can be fully trusted. We can place our full weight down on the reality of *who* He is and *what* He has said.

It amazes me that the same leaders who are totally confident to tell you that God has a *plan* for your life often strongly oppose the teaching that God has a *person* for your life as well. They would be totally fine if I wrote a book about how God has a career path that was pre-planned just to fit you, but they are offended that I would suggest He has a person so sovereignly selected as well. This may seem disconnected, but I am beginning to see that many in the ministry world have allowed the glorification of career over family!

Some leaders have warned me about the dangers of proclaiming that God has a perfect match for people. They tell me that if someone ends up being single their whole life, they will resent me (or God) because they were told there was someone for them. I can assure you that this is not my intention.

This chapter is not designed to be defensive, and I have tried to not make the tone sound that way. But in light of all of the discouraged singles who would be transformed by these oft-repressed truths, I must clarify how sad it is that they have been hidden from the many because of the few.

Inferential Theology

I want to share something with you that could vastly help to simplify your relationship with the LORD: We do not have to imagine every possible scenario of how a truth could play out to determine if it is true or not.

I believe there is a danger in ministry called "inferential theology." I am defining this as the idea that if one thing is true, then something must also be true, and then that would mean something else must be true. In other words, this type of thinking takes one truth and "infers" a thousand other things from it.

Instead of interpreting scripture with scripture (2 Peter 1:20), this kind of theology interprets scripture with experiences. People who do this often focus on "but what about" situations. These could be things they have read in books or even situations they may personally know about. The focus becomes on what God *didn't* do for someone, and they filter and shape a whole theology around that.

They essentially "throw the baby out with the bathwater" and say that if it is not true in *this particular person's experience*, then we cannot say it is true at all!

For example, some people challenge the idea that God makes perfect matches today because they know of someone who is still waiting for one. They say, "if this theology is true, then what about this person?"

Now please hear my heart, experiences do matter in life. We are not supposed to ignore our experiences. But in the same way that we should not be led solely by our emotions, we should also not be led solely by our experiences! How should we be led? The Bible says that we are to be led "by the Spirit" (Romans 8:14).

The point is, we must live like what God has said trumps how we feel and what we have seen. We are supposed to learn from experiences, and emotions are supposed to serve us—but neither of them should be authoritative in our lives.

Something can be true even if it does not *feel* true to us. Something can be true even if it is not true in *our experience*.

The Bible says that Jesus is "*the* Truth" (John 14:6). Notice the article "the" and the capital "T" on Truth. That means He is the Truth *supreme*. Yet millions of people die every day without knowing Jesus. He was neither true in how they *felt* nor in their *experience* (based on their perceptions, of course). So I'm saying, let's not determine what is true simply from human perceptions, feelings, or experiences. Let us base what is true on what God has *said*.

And while I will share a great deal of experience in this book, my sole focus is on what *God has said* about meeting your deepest desires as you learn to delight in Him!

You Can't Say That...

People used inferential theology against Paul. He shared such a profound truth that "where sin abounds, grace abounds all the more" (Romans 5:20). And then people said something like, "You can't say that because if *that* is true then it must *also* be true that sinning more would get us more grace. You are going to lead people to sin more!" But what did Paul say? "Good point?" No! He said, "God forbid! How shall we, that are dead to sin, live any longer therein?" (Romans 6:2, KJV).

The point he was making is that truth doesn't need to be worked out into all of its possible ramifications before it can be accepted, believed, and get this—*proclaimed*!

Paul was not afraid of being misunderstood, and his teaching did not focus on "what ifs."

Let me say it this way, *exceptions* are never the *rule!*

We have to be very careful as leaders to not base our teaching and even prophecy on the fear of exceptions!

If we are making our decisions based on the fear of misinterpretation, we are less likely to be led by the Holy Spirit to boldly speak the truth in love.

What If?

All that being said, some pushback I have received from faith leaders comes from genuine concern for the people who may misunderstand.

I care about these people too, so I want to be as clear as possible. As best as I can, I would like to prevent the misapplication of the teachings in this book.

So let me give you the top three concerns I have heard voiced by those who are hesitant to embrace what I call the "perfect match theology" and see if I can clear them up by interpreting truth with truth.

1) What if someone has the gift of singleness (or stays single for the rest of their life)?

We must let the truth of scripture speak for itself. The scriptures are clear that *some* are given the gift of singleness (1 Corinthians 7:7).

Paul even said I wish you were *all* like me—single (1 Corinthians 7:7). But what's his point? They are *not*. Most of them were not like Paul and given the gift of singleness but given the gift of the perfect match.

53

So singleness is a gift for *some,* but *the majority* of people in this world have not been given the gift of singleness but the gift of a perfect match.

If we are so afraid of misleading people (even though the examples of perfect matches are clear in scripture) because they might have the gift of singleness, we will never prepare people for their match when they do come along! That is setting them up for failure.

We get into dangerous waters when we start basing our theology on the exceptions we have seen. Living by exceptions is dangerous!

Think of it more practically. Unemployment is an unfortunate reality in our country. But since not everyone is going to get a job, do we start preparing people to live unemployed so they are not offended if the right job never comes along? Do we tell them to not get their hopes up? Do we prepare the majority for what only the minority will experience?

The gift of singleness frightens many single people. Some even think that God might use it as a punishment. The majority of people I have counseled over the years who were single and feared that God had resigned them to lifelong singleness were *totally wrong.* As time went on, they found out that God *did* have someone for them after all. They were afraid that they would be alone for the rest of their lives, but that did not happen.

Sadly, they lived in fear for many years when they didn't need to! And you know what? I think a lot of their fears came from "exception" teaching because with that kind of thinking you can never be certain about anything. Being confident is interpreted as pride or presumption, so countless disciples are left to be "tossed to and fro by the waves" (Ephesians 4:14, ESV).

These leaders make others in their image. They are "always learning and never able to arrive at a knowledge of the truth" (2 Timothy 3:7, ESV).

Could singleness be something God has for a person and they just need to submit? Sure—but remember—God *wants* to give us the desire of our hearts (Psalm 37:4). So while it's important to surrender our will to His, He is not some absent Father who tests us by constantly making our desires and our realities clash. Yes, there are times for self-denial, but I believe the greater reality is the abundant life which Jesus came to provide (John 10:10). I have met many people who are acutely focused on a life of self-denial, hardship, and suffering but are missing the abundant, spacious, gracious gifts God wants to provide them.

I'd also like to propose that to a person surrendered to God's will, the gift of singleness will actually feel like that—a gift! Something we open up and are *thankful* for.

> *Which of you, **if your son asks for bread, will give him a stone?** Or if he asks for a fish, will give him a snake? If you, then, though you are evil, know how to give good gifts to your children, **how much more** will your Father in heaven **give good gifts** to those who ask Him!* **Matthew 7:9-11**

It's not in God's nature to give us a bad or ill-fitting gift. It's not in His nature to give us the *opposite* of our desires. He knows how to give good gifts. So when you open *His* gifts you never have to *pretend* that you like them.

If you have believed a lie about God that He is punishing you or keeping you single for life against your desires, I would encourage you to change your mind (repent). That's not the God of the Bible; that's the God that people who focus on exceptions create in their minds.

My wife has a friend who seems to have the gift of singleness. She has a calling on her life and literally no desire to settle down with a husband. In fact, she was dating someone in college who really wanted to marry her but the thought of becoming a wife was off-putting to her, and she ended the relationship!

I guess you could think of it like feeling the way you might feel about being single the rest of your life but instead feeling that way about marriage. So she has embraced the gift she has been given and pursued her calling full on!

My point here is that desire matters to God. We don't have to live in fear that God is going to dump a gift on us that we don't want! Sure, He doesn't have to do it *our* way. But no matter what, His gift will be what's *best* for us.

I believe that God can give us perfect peace no matter if we have the gift of singleness or are waiting on our perfect match.

God cares *deeply* about our desires. Anyone who says otherwise isn't viewing God as a good Father. Good fathers *delight* in fulfilling the healthy desires of their children.

My wife also has two great aunts (one is now deceased) who felt called to singleness and loved it—never desiring a husband. They lived together as sisters their entire lives and did great things for the LORD. They had a faith community around them and a huge loving family. They were single but not alone because it's *not good* to be alone.

Most importantly—they never viewed their singleness as a *punishment* but as a *gift*. Let's not let the exception be the rule in our theology!

The next exception is something that I want to make crystal clear as to what I am advocating for and what I am not suggesting in this book.

2) What if a married person reads your book and questions if they married the wrong person?

First of all, I'd like to say that if you are married, I'd like you to stop reading the book after this section unless you are reading to help someone who is not married. This book was *not* written for married people but for people who are seeking a spouse.

If you are married, there are two things I want you to know:

First of all, your spouse is the one for you.

> *Therefore what God has joined together, let* **no one** *separate.* **Mark 10:9**

Jesus said that after you are married, *no* one should separate you—not even *the* one!

Hypothetically, let's just say that the person you married was 50th on the list of the right people for you. (By the way, I don't believe such a list like this exists. This is just to illustrate.) When you married them and made those vows before God, *they actually became number one.* They bypass everyone else and are now the top person on the list.

My point is that even if you *think* you should've married someone else, the *power of the vow* promotes them to number one. There is no other "one" than your spouse. Breaking that vow to find a better match will not undo the vow! Countless marriages have been destroyed because Satan whispered the lie that there was someone "else" or "better" to be with. Let me say it clearly: Your spouse is your match!

This is all a way of trying to put God's sovereignty into words. We simply cannot explain everything, but based on what Jesus said, you are supposed to *stay* married and begin viewing them as "the one."

Since we are so focused on exceptions right now, I want to make clear that I am not suggesting you stay in an abusive relationship. Please don't misunderstand.

What I am saying is that *there should be no thought in your mind that you missed the right one.* Breaking your vows would actually be forsaking the right one for the wrong one.

Have you ever thought about why Jesus said that it's wrong to divorce and remarry (Matthew 19:9)? It's because you break your vow which solidified "the one."

In other words, it appears to me that *vows made before God have the power to alter your destiny.*

The good news is that since God is all-powerful, He can make your marriage an incredible match. God is the God of redemption!

> **He** has made everything beautiful in its time.
> **Ecclesiastes 3:11**

The most powerful reality you could accept about your marriage is that *only God* can make it beautiful. But He will not force His way on anyone. You have to *let Him* make your marriage beautiful.

Second of all, never develop a theology to get yourself off the hook.

God's Word is clear—He *hates* divorce (Malachi 2:16).

Jesus never said that divorce happens because you married the *wrong* person.

Do you know what He said is the *real* cause of most divorces?

> Jesus replied, "Moses permitted you to divorce your wives **because your hearts were hard.** But it was not this way from the beginning." **Mathew 19:8**

Hard hearts! We want it our way. We want the other person to change. We want to "find someone better."

The true motives of our hearts are exposed when God asks us to *stay* in a less-than-ideal situation to honor our vows and trust Him. I think that anyone who truly believes in the God of grace and redemption will be committed to God's plan for their marriage, even when it's hard.

You will hear about some of our struggles in marriage later in this book, but suffice it to say—having hard times doesn't mean you married the wrong person!

For more on letting God make your marriage great and to hear about our struggles and lessons in marriage, I suggest you read our forthcoming book called, *Forsaking All Others.*

Let me say it again, we know from the lips of Jesus that people desire divorce because of hard hearts, not because they married the *wrong* person.

So the real question is, would you allow God to expose the hard places in your heart?

Would you talk to Him about the hurt you have experienced and ask Him what He is going to do about it?

It is never a good idea to take matters into our own hands or try to force our way.

Divorced Or Widowed

This is a great time to address those who are divorced or widowed. You may wonder how the theology of the perfect match fits in with you.

First of all, I am truly sorry for your loss. Whether it was through divorce or death, the loss of a spouse is a life-changing event. Even though the *causes* are much different, I am grouping these categories together because there is a lot of similarity in recovery.

Since I have never gone through such emotional trauma, I can only imagine the pain you must be feeling. This was probably someone you were very close to, and now you must adjust to what life looks like without them. More than likely, this was an event that you never saw coming and had very little control over.

But God did.

He saw this from before you were ever born. How do I know that? The Bible says that God has a journal where He has recorded our days—every one of them—before we had lived a single one of them (Psalm 139:16). That's hard to wrap our minds around!

Yet as hard as it is to understand, you must hold on to that truth. God knew about this part of your life before you got married to begin with. Therefore, you can trust Him with the results. And you can be sure that He has a plan for you going forward.

It will only cause you pain and confusion to try to figure out *why* this has happened. The best thing you can do now is focus on what God is *currently* doing. If He knew about this loss in your life long before it happened, then that means He is able to work it together for your good (Romans 8:28).

I am sure there is a great deal of healing that needs to take place when someone loses a spouse. But can I encourage you? Let the Healer make you better and not bitter.

Jesus once said that truly happy people are the ones who are not offended at what He chooses to *do* and what He chooses *not to do* (Matthew 11:6).

Trust that God is so sovereign that He could easily have a perfect match for you after you have moved on from a divorce or the death of a spouse.

My wife and I are friends with a family who has seen a mix of all of these things. The husband, a good friend of mine, has been through a divorce in his past, the loss of his next wife to cancer, and then married his current wife—an amazing woman of God.

This woman was single for over *forty years* before God brought along her perfect match! She continued trusting God that if He desired, she would be married. She *let go* of her plans to God, but she didn't *give up*. She had a strong desire to be married and have children. And when her childbearing years came to an end and she was still single, she had to let that desire go to the LORD as well.

But when she finally met her husband, he had four beautiful little girls who needed a mommy! Even though they would not be able to explain *why* all of the events of the past happened, I am confident they would say that God knew *how* and *when* to bring their perfect match.

So if you are divorced or widowed, my suggestion to you is to ask God what He has for you *now*, trusting that He knew about this ahead of time and certainly will work things together for your good.

The focus of this book is about the thing that God is *currently* doing, in spite of all the past waiting or losses. So look to Him to be your "I AM" (Exodus 3:14) in this moment and seek Him about a perfect match!

To those who fear that married people will abuse this teaching, what I'm saying is simple: does the fact that *married* people don't need to question their match mean that *singles* should not hear this message? No way!

3) What if they never *find* "the one"?

My personal opinion of why people get so upset about saying that there is a specific person for someone is because it creates a whole host of anxiety if not paired with the belief that the same God who *made you for* someone can also *get you to* them.

Any teaching on this subject would be in error if not joined with the amazing truth of God's sovereignty.

Yes, this teaching could create extreme anxiety if you think your perfect match may be in Russia while you are in America. But that kind of thinking is as if God has done all this legwork to create the perfect match for you and then just sits back and says, "Good luck finding them!"

It's completely against the nature of God and the compassionate Father we read about in the New Testament.

I once heard a pastor preach against the belief that God has a perfect match for you simply because that person could live in another country and you may never meet. Doesn't this seem like a theology rooted in man-made thinking? At the bare minimum, I feel that it strongly limits God's power and relegates Him to someone who has no ability to influence our circumstances.

God is all-powerful!

What I am talking about in this book may best be seen in hindsight, not foresight. We can all look back on our lives and see times where it seems like God's hand was at work guiding us or bringing something to pass. I think that God's sovereignty is hard to predict but clear in reverse. Just because we cannot always see it beforehand doesn't mean it will not happen. We must *trust* God to bring His plan to pass.

For example, I can look back now and see that *for sure* I was supposed to be with my wife Korie. There's not a doubt in my mind. I can see God's sovereignty in guiding me to Korie way more *now* than I could when I was afraid to break up with Ashley and be alone for an unknown period of time.

But many times we are not sure if God will work on someone else's behalf the way that He has for us. Some of my closest married friends have agreed that looking backward they know that God carefully orchestrated their match. They are confident that their spouse was exactly the person God designed for them. But they are hesitant to say that God will do it for someone else.

I can understand their hesitancy, but I believe that we don't have to be afraid that God will not come through.

Once you couple the belief of God having a perfect match for you with God being in control and able to "work all things together for your good" (Romans 8:28), you can walk in *freedom*.

When God made Eve for Adam, he didn't say, "Now go out and find the match. She could be anywhere on the planet. Good luck!" Instead, what did God do?

He brought her to the man. Genesis 2:22

The point *isn't* that there's nothing required on your part. The point *is* that God's perfect match *for* your life cannot be detached from His perfect sovereignty *in* your life.

We don't need to fear the exceptions or give a million caveats; we simply need to place our trust in the God who is so sovereign that He can bring our perfect match to us without any intervention on our part at all.

And that's what the next chapter is all about...

04
Free to Let Go

Take delight in the LORD, and He will give you the desires of your heart. **Psalm 37:4**

As I mentioned, this verse is pivotal for finding your perfect match.

God wants to give you the desires of *your* heart. But when we have a promise from God and a desire in our hearts, it is very easy to become obsessed with the fulfillment of that promise.

If you have been single for any length of time, I probably don't have to explain to you how easy it is to size up everyone that you meet to determine if they could be a match.

My wife talks about a time in college where she felt like she had to be present at *everything*. Every church function, every extra-curricular activity, every group hangout, every party, every social setting because she was afraid of missing the person God had for her!

She had heard so many stories from friends and mentors about how God brought *their* perfect match into their lives, and the temptation was high for her to try to recreate their story, or at the bare minimum, to make sure she was *fully* available for the perfect match to come along.

She was acting as if God's plan depended on her figuring it out!

I know the feeling because I did the same thing. But it reached a tipping point in her life where she finally talked to God and told Him that she was wearing herself thin by trying to be everywhere all the time. She told God that if He had someone for her, then it was *up to Him* to bring that person into her life.

I'm sure God couldn't have agreed more! She didn't have to be at every event or make sure she didn't miss her destiny.

The pressure was off.

She embraced the freedom to let go, and that made all the difference in the world.

The Fear Of Missing Out

My wife jokes about how previously, if her friend had met some guy at a soccer game, she felt like she should start going to soccer games to not miss her match—and she hates soccer!

This is true in so many venues. I know from my college days that the "soccer field" for many people is actually the bar. That was where you went looking for a future spouse. And if you didn't go, you felt like you were missing this huge social occasion to meet the right person.

But let's be honest. If you are someone who wants to be "all-in" for God and His plan in your life, it's hard for me to think that the *best* place to find your spouse is in a bar!

By the way, I'm not denying that great marriages have met in the craziest of locations. What I am saying is that *you don't have to force it!* You don't have to go to all of these places and lower your standards for your match to come along.

That's the amazing freedom we find in Psalm 37:4. Our focus isn't supposed to be on obtaining our desires but on learning to delight ourselves—our entire being—in the LORD.

Knowing who I am in Christ and experiencing God's love must come first. I know more than anyone the temptation to chase our inheritance instead of chasing God.

What I'm learning is that *identity and intimacy precede inheritance.* I must be grounded as a son of God (identity) and content with my relationship with Him (intimacy) before I am ready to inherit what He has promised (inheritance).

The freedom to let go comes from this reality: *When we make Him our delight, He fulfills our desires!*

Notice that Psalm 37:4 doesn't say that God *changes* our desires. We have already touched on this a bit, but I get a little annoyed when I hear in Christian circles that God *only* wants to change our desires before He fulfills them.

Look, I understand that when we truly delight ourselves in the LORD we begin to see things the way He sees them and want what He wants. That is awesome! But let's not embrace a poverty theology where we repress every desire we have because, "If we want it, it must be bad!" Far from it!

Jesus made it clear that our Father in heaven is not constantly trying to change our desires:

> *Which of you fathers, if your son asks for a fish, will give him a snake instead?* **Luke 11:11**

Teachings about God giving you the *opposite* of your desires is why so many people are afraid they will never find the right person. But that doesn't view God as a good Father!

Many people have a desire in their hearts, but they just can't fully trust that God *wants* to fulfill it. Psalm 37:4 has no words of warning or clarification to make us think otherwise. It is God's way of saying to put *Him* first and the *rest* will follow.

Jesus intensified this reality when He said:

> Seek **first** His Kingdom and His righteousness, and **all these things** will be given to you as well. **Matthew 6:33**

But wait. What were the "all these things" that Jesus was saying would be given to us? If you look back at the passage, you'll see that he was talking about *material things:* food, water, and clothing (Matthew 6:31).

Many ministry leaders today would be so afraid to say this! They would fear that if they promised the same and the people didn't get all of those things, they would be offended or hurt. But why would we try to protect God's image by *watering down* what He has said or *padding the results*? He is faithful! Don't be afraid to have faith.

Here was Jesus' only warning:

> For the pagans **run after** all these things, and your heavenly Father knows that you need them. **But seek first** His kingdom and His righteousness, and all these things will be given to you as well. **Matthew 6:32-33**

He says that pagans *run after* all these things. But then in another breath, He says not to worry because God will give them to you!

What's His point? His point is that the desires are not wrong, but "running after all these things" is the problem. We are supposed to seek first His kingdom (another way of saying to delight ourselves in God). When He becomes our delight, then we are freed up to receive the desires that would have formerly enslaved us if we had dedicated our lives to obtaining them.

I must admit, the sad reality is that I often delight in my desires instead of delighting in the LORD. It's easy to wake up and focus instantly on getting my list of tasks done and stepping closer to obtaining my goals.

So having the desires isn't wrong, but when my desires become my delight instead of God, there's a great chance that I will miss out on both the desires *and* the LORD. But when the LORD becomes my delight, I get *both!*

The incredible truth I want you to see in this chapter is simply this: When we delight ourselves in God, *He is the One* who brings our desires to pass.

God's Sovereignty On Full Display

The LORD will fulfill His purpose for me.
Psalm 138:8 ESV

God is the One who will fulfill His purpose for you! This should totally eliminate the fear of missing out in your life.

There are so many examples of this in the Bible—especially when it comes to God bringing about our perfect match.

We could talk about how it was in the context of Ruth's daily responsibilities that God brought about her match, Boaz.

We could talk about how Esther ascended to the most royal of relationships not by trying to force her way but by submitting to the long (and painful) process of purification.

We could talk about how the entire model for the body of Christ is marriage and that He perfectly fits the parts together!

But I'd like to tell you about the Biblical account that changed my life...

Isaac And Rebekah

This story was so instrumental in my wife and me finding one another that we named our firstborn son Isaac!

The funny thing is, Isaac doesn't appear as a character until the end of the story when his bride miraculously shows up on his doorstep—which drives home the point of this entire chapter.

> *Abraham was now very old, and the Lord had blessed him in every way. He said to the* **senior servant** *in his household, the one in charge of all that he had, "Put your hand under my thigh. I want you to swear by the Lord, the God of heaven and the God of earth, that you will not get a wife for my son from the daughters of the Canaanites, among whom I am living, but will go to my country and my own relatives and* **get a wife for** *my son Isaac."*
> **Genesis 24:1-4**

So right here we see that Abraham (who is a picture of God the Father in this passage) actually cares *very much* about who his son marries. He has an opinion! What's striking is,

Abraham doesn't send Isaac to pick his own match, but a "senior servant." You'll see the grand symbolism of what's going on here in a bit, but it's important to note that Abraham didn't want Isaac to pick someone based on his own emotions in the heat of the moment. So he sent his most trusted servant to choose wisely.

> The servant asked him, "What if the woman is unwilling to come back with me to this land? Shall I then take your son back to the country you came from?" "**Make sure** that you do **not** take my son back there," Abraham said. **Genesis 24:5-6**

It's clear that Abraham believed there were some who were *not right* for his son!

> "The Lord, the God of heaven, who brought me out of my father's household and my native land and who spoke to me and promised me on oath, saying, 'To your offspring I will give this land'—He will send His angel before you so that you can get a wife for my son from there. **If the woman is unwilling** to come back with you, then you will be released from this oath of mine. Only do not take my son back there." So the servant put his hand under the thigh of his master Abraham and swore an oath to him concerning this matter. **Genesis 24:7-9**

Abraham believes entirely that God has a person for Isaac, so he tells the servant that he can be completely released from his oath if the woman is unwilling to come back. Add to that the mystery that Abraham somehow knows God is going to send an angel ahead of him so that he can find the right spouse for Isaac—and what we see is a man of faith!

That is why Abraham is often called the "father of faith" (Romans 4:16). Even though he had his fair share of mistakes, He took God at His word, even when the odds were not in his favor. This is what you must do as well!

I love that God identifies us by our faith and not our doubt. Abraham is not remembered for the times he messed up but for his great steps of faith. We must see ourselves the same way that God sees us.

Our *future* is not determined by our *past* but by our *God.*

Don't be held back by past failures, keep your focus on your *current* walk with God. Live by faith in Him not faith in your abilities. You will soon feel the freedom that comes from letting go in trust.

Unforced Destiny

Look at what Abraham says to the servant, "If the woman is unwilling to come back with you" (Genesis 24:8). What does this tell us? It shows us that *God never overrides our free will!*

He doesn't force His plan on anyone. Rebekah had a choice! We see a powerful interplay here of God's sovereignty and our own free will.

The Right One At The Right Time

The story continues...

> *Then the servant left, taking with him ten of his master's camels loaded with all kinds of good things from his master. He set out for Northwest Mesopotamia and made his way to the town of Nahor. He had the camels kneel down near the well outside the town;* **it was toward evening,** *the time the women go out to draw water.* **Genesis 24:10-11**

The sun is setting on the opportunity for this servant to find the right match.

I suppose it could be argued that he could just find last-minute lodging and try again tomorrow, but it seems purposeful that these details were recorded.

If you feel that you are almost out of time to find a spouse, fear not! The sun may be setting in a sense, but never let the external circumstances make you doubt God's ability to carry out His plan for your life!

Some of the most incredible movements of God in history came at what seemed like the last possible second. I know in my own life, it felt like I was already out of time to end one relationship and still find my match. But God showed that time is never a problem for Him!

> *Then he prayed, "Lord, God of my master Abraham, make me successful today, and show kindness to my master Abraham. See, I am standing beside this spring, and the daughters of the townspeople are coming out to draw water. May it be that when I say to a young woman, 'Please let down your jar that I may have a drink,' and she says, 'Drink, and I'll water your camels too'—**let her be the one You have chosen** for Your servant Isaac. By this, I will know that You have shown kindness to my master."*
> **Genesis 24:12-14**

This is so huge: "Let her be *the one* you have chosen!"

Wait, so there is a *one*!

The one *who* had chosen? God!

My point isn't for you to seek a sign from God or to ask your parents to arrange a marriage. My point is that there undeniably *was* a one!

For those who fear this kind of teaching, you have to at least admit that in *this particular case* there was *"the one"* that God had for Isaac. You could deem that this is an exception, but I don't believe that we see any attempt by God to warn us that this is so!

> *Before he had finished praying, Rebekah came out with her jar on her shoulder. She was the daughter of Bethuel son of Milkah, who was the wife of Abraham's brother Nahor. The woman was **very beautiful, a virgin; no man had ever slept with her.** She went down to the spring, filled her jar and came up again.* **Genesis 24:15-16**

The Waiting Ends

In case you couldn't predict what happened next, let me summarize: She was *the one* for Isaac!

What the servant prayed came about. And by the way, she was amazing. We know from these verses that she was a beautiful woman, had kept herself pure, and had strong character. God was gracious to show the servant the perfect match for Isaac. She came and offered to water the camels, and the servant took her up on that offer. The servant meets her parents and explains why he has come. The parents basically can't decide if she should go.

> *Then they said, "Let's call the young woman and ask her about it." So they called Rebekah and asked her, "Will you go with this man?" "**I will go,**" she said.* **Genesis 24:57-58**

Again, we see that God's sovereignty doesn't manipulate our free will. It is so important to know that Rebekah had a choice! So even within the context of God designing a person for us, He never violates our free will.

Thankfully, He is faithful to redeem our past and protect us from derailing our destiny. These two pieces of God's sovereignty and our free will are so intricate—and I do not pretend to understand how they work together. Many books can (and have) been written about this. The focus of this book is not "*how* it all happens" but "*that* it happens!"

God is the Perfect Matchmaker. We don't have to figure Him out to *trust* Him!

Bear in mind that this meant she decided to marry a man she had *never met!* Talk about trusting God. She packs her bags and heads to meet this man.

> *Then Rebekah and her attendants got ready and mounted the camels and went back with the man. So the servant took Rebekah and left.* **Genesis 24:61**

I wonder what that ride was like for Rebekah. First of all, who knows how long it took for their caravan to make it there. *More waiting.*

But more importantly, what was she thinking? Was she like, "What the heck did I just sign up for?" I mean, at the bare minimum, she had to be wondering if he was good looking or not. What if he was a terrible person? A bad kisser? She had never met him! She could've wrestled with all of these things and more.

I would imagine at some point on this journey, Rebekah had to give these fears over to the LORD and trust that God had her best in mind.

There were *plenty* of reasons for her to be concerned. But *one* fact trumped all of those reasons: *God is on the throne.*

Rebekah represents a woman of faith who was willing to trust her God more than her fears. She did not allow the fear of the unknown to delay her destiny.

Here's the best part—*her waiting finally ended, and none of her fears came to fruition.*

> *Now Isaac had come from Beer Lahai Roi, for he was living in the Negev. He went out to the field **one evening to meditate,** and **as he looked up**, he saw camels approaching. **Rebekah also looked up** and saw Isaac. She got down from her camel and asked the servant, **"Who is that man** in the field coming to meet us?"* **Genesis 24:62-65**

Translation: Is that stud over there my future husband?

> *"He is my master," the servant answered. So she took her veil and covered herself. Then the servant told Isaac all he had done. Isaac brought her into the tent of his mother Sarah, and he married Rebekah. **So she became his wife, and he loved her;** and Isaac was comforted after his mother's death.* **Genesis 24:65-67**

This was an amazing ending to the story, and God was the author!

Letting Go In Trust

Let me ask you a question. What did Isaac and Rebekah have to do to meet one another?

I mean, let's be honest. Did either of them take a proactive role in finding their future spouse?

If you truly grasp the depth of this story, you have to admit— neither one of them did much of anything! God brought a divine moment into the midst of their ordinary lives. In fact, Rebekah was just going about her daily tasks and getting water from a well when all this came to pass.

She was willing to follow God's leading by being a servant to a stranger. That speaks more to her character than to any planning on her part! She couldn't have possibly known that this stranger held the key to her destiny.

All Isaac had to do was meditate, rest, and fellowship with God until God brought it to pass!

When Rebekah shows up, Isaac is meditating in the field. Think about that! We don't even know if Isaac was aware that his father had sent the servant on this mission in the first place. Maybe he had no idea what was going on and then—boom—his bride shows up on his doorstep!

One day, God brought it all to pass.

All they had to do was "look up" (Genesis 24:63-64).

All of this was going on in the background, apart from their knowledge.

But so often we want to take it out of the *background* and put it in the *foreground*—making it our primary focus and pursuit instead of resting in our relationship with the LORD.

I'd like to encourage you about the powerful implications this has for your life. Isaac goes from one day just sitting in a field to immediately married! God can make it that easy and fast for you as well but you must be willing to let go of it all to Him.

Look, I don't mean to imply that there is nothing required on your part or that you should never go out in public again. In fact, I dedicate a whole chapter later in this book about all the things you can be doing *right now* to pave the way for your match. But the truth is, until you embrace the theology that it is *God's* job to bring about your perfect match, you won't be able to enjoy your life *right now.*

Often we get our minds into planning mode about the future so much that we are unable to enjoy the present. Over time, this kind of bondage can make you totally unprepared to meet your match.

I cannot tell this story about Abraham sending a senior servant to get a bride for his son without mentioning the powerful illustration of the Father sending His Spirit to get a Bride for His Son. Marriage is the exact picture that the New Testament uses to describe our sanctification process now. God the Father sends the Holy Spirit to sanctify a Bride for His Son!

But back to your future spouse—I'd like to suggest to you that it's exactly the same thing. God has gone ahead of you to secure your spouse. Your job isn't to try to make it happen but to let go in trust, believing that God is working on your behalf.

So essentially, stop trying to make it happen! You are free to let go to the God who will bring it to pass in His way and timing.

God Himself will orchestrate your destiny.

And above all, remember, *you need only delight yourself in Him.*

Part II: The Process

05
Single and Hating It

Breakthrough

I'll never forget that moment for the rest of my life.

It had been one week since I ended my relationship with Ashley.

I was on my way to help out my friend Luke, the same one who had endured the crying ride with me earlier. He was getting his new house set up on campus for the coming school year, and he needed my help picking up a new mattress from the store. So he asked if I would meet him there.

This was par for the course; owning a truck at the time made me a prime target to be asked to help transport things. It was to be expected. But what happened during that ride was very *unexpected*.

I pulled up to the stoplight at the intersection of 52 and 350 in my hometown of Lafayette, Indiana. I was in my blue Dodge Dakota pickup truck when suddenly, it happened.

I couldn't have sat there more than a couple of minutes, but it felt like an eternity because of the significance of what happened.

It may seem strange as I try to explain it, but I promise you that what happened in me represented a shift in my identity that forever changed my life.

I suddenly became aware of something inside of me that felt different. It's very hard to put into words the reality of what was going on in my soul, but my best explanation is that I realized that something was gone which had always been there.

As I sat there probing deeper and praying about what this feeling was inside of me, suddenly it dawned upon me—*the need to be with someone was gone!*

It was like I realized that I no longer had something which I had carried for so long—a lack. This emptiness was now full. Not that it never manifested in any way again, but it was truly gone in terms of its permanent place of residence in my life.

When I realized that the need to have a significant other was gone, I started screaming for joy out loud in my truck. Thankfully, I was all alone, but I must say that the joy of what I felt would've drowned out any fear of what others thought. I just kept saying "It's gone! It's gone! Thank You, God!"

A better theological explanation probably would've been, "It's filled! It's filled! The emptiness I have carried for as long as I can remember is gone!"

Across the road at that intersection was a beautiful farmhouse on several acres of land. This house became a little marker or symbol for me of my newfound freedom. Still to this day, when I pass through that intersection, I often look at that house and remember what God did for me.

Sometimes you don't know how much bondage you are under until you are released from the weight you have carried for so long. It's like walking out into the sunshine when you've been inside all day. God set me free from the neediness that was once my permanent prison!

Here's an excerpt from what I wrote in my journal that day:

> *"Tonight on the road driving to pick up Luke's mattress, I had a realization that God took away the fear in my heart of always having to be with someone. God showed me that He broke the chains of my bondage to the lie of Satan that I had to have someone. God showed me that just having Him was enough. What a screaming joy bursting forth from my heart to actually believe for the first time that God alone is all I need. Not just all I need to scrape by, but amazing, fulfilling, and powerfully peaceful beyond anything I've ever known. This has been the most powerful week of my life, and I never want to forget how God showed up right on time and delivered me. He gave me such peace about everything that I was worried about. Thanks be to God on high. He reigns!"*

After I picked up the mattress that day, one of Luke's friends decided to ride back with me. I'll never forget the feeling of that drive. The sun was setting in perfect color. The summer day was fading to a cool evening. I had Christian music on the radio, and the whole way home I kept saying out loud, "It's such a great day. What a great day. Man, such a nice day." My riding companion didn't say much, but I felt so much peace during that ride, continuing to rejoice that my former void was now filled.

And here's the thing: I was *single*. God showed me how to enjoy the season of singleness!

We are not supposed to hate the season we are in. Certainly, some seasons require more endurance than others, but God wants us to be able to walk as whole individuals *today*. We don't have to wait for some date in the future to begin walking in an intimate relationship with Him.

I realized something that day that I wish I would've known many years before: *Until we are content with God alone, we are ultimately delaying our destiny.*

He Fulfills When We Delight

> *Take delight in the LORD, and **He** will give you the desires of your heart.* **Psalm 37:4**

We are not done with this verse yet!

If something holds the number one spot for our affections more than God Himself, we cannot legitimately say that we are delighting ourselves (our entire beings) in Him.

Last chapter we talked about how we are free to let go so God can bring about our desires—that it's not on us to bring them to fruition. But the corollary to that statement is found in the same verse. While we must wait on and trust in God to fulfill our desires, *He is under no obligation to do so until we make Him our delight.*

At first glance this can seem cruel, but it must be understood that without making God our highest affection, anything He gives us has the potential to harm us instead of bless us. We can easily find our identity in the thing (or person) instead of in Him.

Hopefully it's obvious that I'm not saying you have to be perfect before God will bring along your perfect match. Not at all! But the reality is, God doesn't want to give you something prematurely for which you are not ready. And it's almost as if the switch to engage our destinies is making God our supreme delight.

This does not mean we pretend like we don't *have* desires. In light of this verse, the truth has to be that we are *able* to simultaneously make the LORD our delight while also stewarding desires in our hearts! But we must learn the difference between desires and neediness.

While we don't need to repress our desires, God definitely can show us how to live with complete contentment while we wait on Him to bring His plan to pass in our lives.

We must view these seasons of waiting as seasons of preparation. And if part of the preparation God does is teaching us how to delight in Him, it stands to reason that we could delay the fulfillment of the promise simply by resisting the process.

So if you are bound and determined to find a mate, you may be missing the preparation which would allow God to bring about your destiny. It's really counterproductive.

Filled By His Fullness

Paul described Jesus this way:

> *The fullness of Him who fills everything in every way.* **Ephesians 1:23**

The English Standard Version says, *"the fullness of Him who fills **all in all.**"*

This is where we get the saying that God must be our "all in all." He is must be our all (everything) *in* all (everything).

He is able to fill everything and never run out. The true answer to our emptiness, singleness, loneliness (really any "ness") is Jesus Christ.

He is the Perfect Husband. In other words, until you let Jesus fill every void in your life, you will keep coming up empty.

In his letter to the Colossians, Paul gives us some insight about Jesus filling our emptiness:

> *He is **before all things,** and **in Him all things hold together.** Colossians 1:17*

So until He is *before* all things to you in rank, order, and priority—including *before finding a spouse*—then you cannot expect Him to hold your plans and relationships together!

As hard as it may be to hear, the reality is that if you are not satisfied now, you will absolutely *not* be satisfied when you are married.

One of the most important things my wife and I teach in premarital counseling is to not look to your spouse to give you what only God can. We often put people in the role of God and ask them to fill needs that only He can fill.

When we allow others to have a place of magnitude in our life which belongs to God, that's called idolatry.

I cannot tell you how many singles I have met who have shifted from simply preparing for a spouse to actually idolizing a spouse. It's all they can think about, and it's become such a place of priority (another way of saying "before all things") that even spending an evening alone is torture for them.

So they flood themselves with busyness and "opportunities" to meet someone, and they live like they cannot find *peace* until they find a *spouse*. While this manifests in so many ways, it has never been truer than when it comes to the addiction of pornography.

When we create an idol in our hearts, we will do whatever we have to do to obtain it—even with false intimacy. I can't tell you how many men I have counseled who wrote off their addictions because they thought that the addiction would go away once they got married.

They had no idea that their behavior actually represented a void in their hearts which only Christ Himself could fill—and was completely willing to fill. How do I know this? Because only Jesus has the capacity to fill *all in all.*

Sometimes it seemed like their choice to view pornography was an attempt to pay God back for making them wait so long for a spouse! They rationalized their dysfunction by saying that it was only temporarily filling a need. They excused their present idolatry thinking it would change when they could "legitimately" get that need met!

Can I tell you something? Whether it's pornography, vanity, or the insecurity of constantly looking for a spouse—that addiction will only be *intensified* by marriage. If it's not dealt with now, it could wreak havoc against your future.

Every need. Every desire. Every longing in our hearts is fulfilled in Jesus. That's called, "delighting ourselves in the LORD." The amazing thing is that it *paves the way* for God to give us the desires of our hearts.

Truth be told, many of us are chasing desires and thinking that we will delight ourselves in God once He gives us what we want. But that is never the case. Not only is that putting the cart before the horse—it's putting the harvesting before the planting.

If we aren't satisfied in God now, we won't be when we are married. Anyone who has ever been privy to the financial giving numbers in a church knows this principle. So many people *say* that once they have money they will give more generously. But the reality is that if you don't give generously when you have a little, you won't when you have a lot!

So if you are trying to find satisfaction through lust, thinking it's only a temporary relief to a problem—guess what? When you get married and the highs of the honeymoon wear off, the lust problem can actually become amplified.

That's where many guys give up and succumb to even worse things like adultery or substance abuse because the solution they set their hearts on has failed them!

> For ***from His fullness*** we have all received, grace upon grace. **John 1:16 ESV**

The point is that the solution to all of our emptiness is *real intimacy* with Jesus Christ.

And *from that place of fullness,* we can have an amazing relationship with someone else.

It is just like how we can't give away something we don't have. We cannot love someone if our bank account of love is empty to begin with.

The bottom line is that you've got to become a person committed to contentment *now,* or you will only bring baggage into your marriage *later.*

And if you think that finding a spouse will make the emptiness you feel go away, you are in for a rude awakening!

The emptiness and insecurity we feel cannot be filled by any other person or thing.

So here's my question: What would it look like for you to come into your perfect match *already full?*

Full Before You Find

Let me paint a picture of what your life could be like if you were full *before* you found your match. Here are 15 ways to be secure in Christ before you meet your match:

1) Don't interpret alone time as time alone.

Ask God to show you how to be content even when there's no one else around. Learn to be at peace when there's nothing to do, nowhere to go, and no one to see. Oh yeah—and no Facebook or smartphone to nervously search. This may seem harsh, but if you are not comfortable with yourself, it means you are not satisfied with God.

> *In **quietness and trust** is your strength.*
> **Isaiah 30:15**

2) Ask Jesus to show you how *He* is the Perfect Husband.

Spend time in His Presence and talk to Him about your commitment to Him above any earthly man or woman.

> ***The bride belongs to the bridegroom.*** *The friend who attends the bridegroom waits and listens for him, and is full of joy when he hears the bridegroom's voice. That joy is mine, and it is now complete.* **John 3:29**

Would you be satisfied with your current level of intimacy with God for the rest of your life?

If God never gave you a spouse, would your relationship with Him fall apart?

These questions are very revealing about your level of fullness with God. Remember, if preparation is key, then your intimacy with God will be part of determining the quality of your relationship with your spouse.

3) Don't seek validation from the opposite sex.

It is so important to not try to fill insecurity with the wrong things. Ask God to show you what He thinks about you. Research the scriptures about who God says you are. (A great place to start would be the book of Ephesians.)

Your focus as a single should be on who God says you are and nothing else. I see far too many singles getting their emotional fulfillment from members of the opposite sex.

4) Shift your focus from what you lack to what you possess.

> *Finally, brothers and sisters, whatever is true, whatever is noble, whatever is right, whatever is pure, whatever is lovely, whatever is admirable—if **anything** is excellent or praiseworthy—**think about such things.** **Philippians 4:8***

We are never told in scripture to focus on our flaws or weaknesses or what we lack. If you are constantly thinking about how you come up short, you can be sure that Satan is whispering in your ear. God doesn't want you to have a single ounce of self-hatred or negativity. Even if there are things about you that you want to change, it doesn't help to dwell on them. The Bible teaches that we become what we focus on (Genesis 30:37-43, Proverbs 23:7, Romans 12:2).

5) Learn to enjoy your life as it is currently—at this very moment—today.

> *This is the day that the LORD has made; let us rejoice and be glad in it.* **Psalm 118:24 ESV**

Be present in the moment and bask in the goodness of what God is giving you. Don't focus on what God *isn't* doing for you—keep your mind only on what He *is* doing. I suggest making thankful lists whether written, verbal, or mental every day. Gratitude is healing balm to our souls.

Let every day be a day to recognize God's sovereignty in your life. "This is the day the LORD has made, *I will rejoice* and be glad *in it*." This means that it is a choice you make!

If God designed this day for you, all you have to do is be glad in it. He is in control. Appreciate the gift of life for another day.

We are not told to just grit our teeth through today and rejoice some far off day in the future when everything lines up perfectly. No, *today* is the day God has made for us. We are supposed to be glad in *it*.

6) Stop picturing your life as "incomplete" until the perfect match comes along.

> *There is a time for everything and a season for every activity under the heavens.* **Ecclesiastes 3:1**

Don't put your life on pause because you think you don't have a purpose until you get married. God has a purpose for you in *this season* of your life!

God would not have given you this time of singleness if it was not *extremely* valuable for you and the calling on your life. This season is shaping you for your destiny.

There is a time for your singleness to end, but for most of you reading, now is not that time. This season is for a special purpose, so don't just try to get through it!

Don't live your life like you are incomplete without a significant other. Honestly, that's not very attractive anyway!

7) Give couples and married people a break.

Don't you hate it when non-single people are like, "Hey enjoy your freedom! You have no responsibilities!" when in reality all you desire is to have someone to whom you *are* responsible?

Many of your friends who aren't single will try to give you advice or help you feel better about your situation. Some of them don't realize how their words may come across. Since *they* have a significant other, it's easy to become bitter toward them thinking, "Yeah, but you have a spouse!"

The truth is, we should desire God's wisdom, even from people who have not experienced what we are going through. God can speak through a donkey (Numbers 22:30), so be humble enough to hear even from people that may not understand what you're going through.

Do you feel insecure around couples or friends who have a significant other?

Learn to rejoice with those who rejoice (Romans 12:15). Just because your friend is happily married doesn't mean that you won't be. Our God has no lack!

8) Stop picturing the worst case scenario for your life.

My times are in Your hands. **Psalm 31:15**

Every time you find yourself fearing that you'll still be alone in 20 years should be a time of repentance for getting ahead of God and not trusting in His timing.

I have found that one of the biggest lies Satan tries to whisper in your ear is actually a question: *Who could ever want me?*

Satan puts this in the first person so that you think it's your own thoughts. Suffice it to say, this is his way of making you doubt the goodness of God who made you to be *you!*

Never believe that God would make something invaluable or that no one could ever want you. That is such a lie!

So if you picture being alone forever or have embraced the lie that no one could ever want you, it's time to *repent*! You read that right. You need to change your mind *now*—before those thoughts become solidified as your own.

Thoughts like these should be quickly identified as a temptation from the enemy to distrust God. God is fully capable of bringing about your match, and He made you— every part of you—with *great* intentionality.

If Satan can get you to hate yourself, he can get you to doubt your destiny!

And how will you walk in faith if you are consumed with doubt? Believing these lies makes you carry yourself in a completely different manner than a son or daughter of God should.

9) Stop sizing up everyone you meet.

It's a really unhealthy practice.

Set your minds *on things above, not on earthly things.* **Colossians 3:2**

When you are not able to engage strangers without picturing if they could be your spouse, it shows that your mind is not set on things above. It actually represents a stronghold in your thought life.

As a single person, it totally makes sense to be aware of people with whom you really hit it off. But many singles find it hard to not size up every single person they meet and imagine how they could be their match. That's not only unhealthy—it's unholy! And it sets you up for a lot of disappointment!

In social settings, do you automatically scan the crowd for your potential mate?

10) Don't ever say, "I give up!"

That would mean you are giving up on God. Yes, you should be at a place of total surrender. But there's a big difference between being surrendered and throwing in the towel.

A surrendered heart knows the difference between giving up and letting go. If you are in a place of despair or frustration, it's likely that you have decided to "give up" instead of "let go" to the plans of the LORD.

I have talked to numerous people, even over the course of writing this book, who have amazing stories of God bringing along their perfect match *at their point of greatest surrender*. They were willing to stay single if that was God's will, and they trusted that God's plan was best.

Sometimes God is waiting for us to trust Him so much that we hand over our plans and desires in exchange for His. And as my friends can testify, that is often when He gives us more than we imagined to begin with!

We should live from a place of surrender—ready to accept with gratitude the Master's plan. But we should not live from a place of defeat—always thinking that God wants us to settle for less than our desires!

God is amazing in His ability to get our hearts to a place where we can receive His best. Often, His *best* is *far better* than we could've ever envisioned. Sometimes that requires God changing our desires, but it always requires us to hold our plans loosely and believe our Father knows best.

So don't give up—let go.

11) Recognize and confess that you will no longer partner with self-pity.

Self-pity is not only unattractive but sinful. It is a stronghold of self-focus which denies God's care for you based on your circumstances. It meditates on thoughts that are opposed to His character.

Self-pity is the same line of thought that Satan tempted Adam and Eve with in the Garden of Eden. He got them to *question God's character* based on what God *wasn't* giving them.

Think about it. To stop delighting in the LORD, your focus must shift back to yourself. One of Satan's greatest tools for doing this is whispering sad tales about your life. When you agree with these thoughts, you are making a false confession about God—believing that He has failed you.

Feeling sorry for yourself leads to an environment of doubt and despair. It may feel good to your *flesh* for a time, but it is destructive to your *soul*. Do not take the bait and shift into an unhealthy focus on your troubles.

Self-pity puts you in a pit so deep that you literally cannot walk in faith because self-pity and faith oppose one another! And since promises are inherited through faith and patience (Hebrews 6:12), I'd say that at best, self-pity is delaying your destiny.

Are you living from a place of self-pity and discouragement or surrender and confidence in God?

12) Start declaring your dependence on God for your needs.

If you cannot be content without being with another person, it inevitably leads to something called "co-dependency." This is where your very worth is determined by the presence and approval of someone else in your life. You feel that you cannot be yourself without them—your identity depends on it. It has also been called, "relationship addiction."

But God calls us to total dependence on Him—not another human.

While the goal of most single people is "finding the one," the best preparation for your future marriage should be to get to the place of total dependence on the LORD.

When we are unwilling to let go of our plans and desires and delight in Him, He often holds back the fruition of our desires because it would not be good for us.

13) Don't try to manipulate God to get what you want.

Another way of saying this is: Don't base your relationship with the LORD on Him bringing you a spouse.

When you are single, the temptation is to treat God more like a genie that you can command instead of your most intimate relationship. So don't try to control God.

The truth is that if your every waking moment with God is all about Him bringing you a spouse, guess what happens to your relationship with Him when you actually get one?! You no longer know how to relate to God because your whole relationship was based on Him giving you your idol. There was no substance!

> *Who has known the mind of the Lord? Or **who has been His counselor? Romans 11:34***

It's a ridiculous thought, really. Can you imagine if God needed a counselor? Who would He go to? Can you picture God lying on a couch while *you* were behind the desk with a clipboard advising *Him* on what to do? Isn't that a ridiculous thought? But that's often how we treat God. We wouldn't *say* it, but we *think* He needs our counsel.

We try to manipulate God in all sorts of ways, from telling Him what to do to even trying to perform so that He will give us what we want!

> *Every good and perfect gift is **from above.*** **James 1:17**

So are you looking above for His gifts or trying to force your own way?

Are you afraid of missing out? Do you border on manipulating and controlling situations, people, or even God to give you the best shot at finding the one?

14) Don't try to figure everything out!

*Trust in the LORD with all your heart and **lean not** on your own understanding.* **Proverbs 3:5**

This verse is probably one of the most well-known, oft-quoted verses in the entire Bible. Yet, I would suggest that it is one of the least-practiced. And I know that from my own life. But God is gracious to remind me in His own way when I am venturing into territory that falls under His job description and capabilities.

Being reminded of this is one of my favorite things because I am someone who likes to know everything before it happens.

But I have found that it usually leads to my own misery to try to figure out how everything is going to go down before it happens.

You see, even trying to figure out His plan could be trying to assert mental control or grab hold of something that God doesn't want you to know yet!

Even trying to figure out why things are taking so long can be futile. You must trust that God has a good reason for *everything* He is allowing in your life.

Believe in His goodness. Trust that you have not missed out.

He will bring about your *perfect match* at the *perfect time*.

This chapter is about God healing the void in your soul, and once that void is healed, you can actually enjoy this season of singleness in your life.

For me personally, *it took being single to be healed*. But I didn't understand that in the moment.

While we will talk about how to prepare for your match in a future chapter, even preparation can be manipulation if not done with the right heart.

So stop trying to figure out everything that God is going to do. Leave it where it belongs—with Him!

15) Seek Jesus as your heart's desire from the very start.

> But **seek first** His kingdom and His righteousness, and all these things will be given to you as well. **Matthew 6:33**

Are you truly delighting yourself in the LORD, or has the idea of finding someone become an idol for you?

Can you really say that you are seeking His Kingdom *first*? Is the LORD your *highest* delight?

These are tough questions to answer honestly.

When your relationship with Christ has first place, you are not going to settle or compromise with a potential spouse.

To make that clear, my wife and I started our first official "date" by spending the first hour separately seeking the LORD.

It may seem cheesy, but after seeing myself attach my identity to another person in the past, I wanted to guard against that ever happening again. At that point in our relationship, it was almost a way of prophesying into our future what our true priorities would be.

We knew that Christ needed to have first place, or we would not make it. And truth be told, there was a ton of insecurity and misplaced priorities that God was happy to shake out along the way.

To hear more about our struggles and lessons about marriage, I suggest you read our forthcoming book, *Forsaking All Others*. That would be another great way to prepare in faith for when God brings along your perfect match.

When Jesus has the place of ultimate priority in your life, you will be grounded for any struggle that comes your way.

God's Perfect Timing

I would like to put all of this in better context by encouraging you. This chapter is about healing the void in your soul so that you are able to enjoy the life God is *currently* giving you until He brings along your perfect match. But if you have been single for years or even decades, some of this can be hard to hear.

I am not suggesting that you are not already doing many or all of these things. Doing the *right* things doesn't guarantee *immediate* results—that would simply be controlling God.

That being said, it *has* to be true that the more you submit to the process and genuinely seek His kingdom first, the more quickly things *could* come about as opposed to resisting His preparation. I use the word "could" because it's not always a matter of *you* being prepared.

It can be a freeing thing to consider that even if you've got all your ducks in a row, God might still be doing things on the other end of the equation that has nothing to do with you.

That's why we will discuss how important it is to be praying for your future spouse even before you meet them.

We wouldn't want God to put us with our perfect match before *we* are ready or before *they* are ready!

And then again, get this, sometimes it's not a matter of either person being fully prepared but simply a specific number of days which God has pre-ordained (for reasons unknown to us, but they must be good reasons).

> *But when the **set time** had fully come, God sent His Son, born of a woman, born under the law.*
> **Galatians 4:4**

The Greek word for "time" here is *"Chronos"*[3] which is simply a number of days. It's where we get our English word "chronological." This literally meant that Jesus didn't come to earth until the pre-determined *number of days* had passed.

In this verse, it shows that it wasn't just about certain *things* happening but a number of *days* passing. Since God doesn't do anything without a purpose, this is just another opportunity to "trust in the LORD with all our heart" and "lean not on our own understanding" (Proverbs 3:5).

Don't Force It

> *Do not arouse or awaken love **until it so desires.***
> **Song of Songs 2:7**

There's something about waiting for God's timing and not forcing it that is instrumental in finding your match.

So it's not like God's saying, "just be a better person and—boom—it will all happen." That would be living under works of the law and simply changing to get what you want.

The ultimate reality is that *some things* in our destiny will not happen until *God thinks* they should. It should encourage you to know that it doesn't ride on you but that the timing is completely in God's hands.

Free yourself from trying to force your destiny into existence. Don't risk prematurely awakening love before it desires.

God knows best.

We must learn to be content with His timing—and the only way to have *true contentment* is to delight in Him! He will give us a contentment which stays for good.

<u>Who Are You Really?</u>

Let me end this chapter by telling you about a powerful dream I had a few years ago. It was about a close male relationship of mine who was struggling to find his purpose in life. I believe that the LORD revealed the main stronghold in his life through this dream.

In the dream, he was about to move to another city trying to find contentment by changing his geography. When he tried to leave, I confronted him by standing in his way and tackling him in the middle of the road.

Then, I stood over him and pointed in his face and said, *"Thus says the LORD: 'Who is _____(I said his name here) if he's not with a woman?'"* And then I woke up.

I shared this dream with him in real life (don't worry, I didn't tackle him). I believe it helped him realize that he was *basing his identity* on being with a significant other.

That was why he couldn't be content where he was because he felt incomplete if he wasn't with someone romantically. So anytime he was rejected by a woman, he would change his entire geography to run from the pain and search for a fix.

I couldn't help but fill in my own name in the question as well: "Who is Wes Raley if he's not with a woman?"

It's a good question. It's a fair question. It's a revealing question. And I suggest you ask yourself the same thing:

Who is _____ if you're not with _____?

When you can honestly answer that question, you'll be on your way to delighting yourself in God and enjoying singleness instead of hating it.

06
Perfect Matches Match

Not With My Match

"I should've never been with her to begin with!" I couldn't believe that I said the words out loud. They hung in the air as I looked around my parents' kitchen making sure no one heard me.

I was sitting there on a summer day in 2010 listening to a podcast by a man named Jon Courson. Somehow I had stumbled upon a message about being with the right person —a message that would change my life.[4]

In that one moment I realized that if I would have known years ago what I heard in that message, I don't think I would've ever started my three year relationship. And truth be told, it would've kept me out of *several* relationships in my younger years.

In all my years of going to church, I had never heard such practical teaching from the Bible about how to find the person God made me for.

That one message changed my life. It was so powerful that I still remember the *three major shifts* in my thinking which God brought about through this man's powerful sermon that day.

1) Perfect matches match.

> *Then the man said, "This **at last** is **bone of my bones** and **flesh of my flesh**; she shall be called Woman, because she was taken out of Man."*
> **Genesis 2:23 ESV**

I love how Adam actually says, "At last!" It portrays exactly how many of us have felt. After trying to find a match among a group that had no matches (animals), Adam was overjoyed to finally find someone who perfectly matched—Eve!

"Bone of my bones and flesh of my flesh" is a Hebrew idiom which essentially means *"we are the same, you and I."*

It would be close to our modern day saying, "We are mirror-images." You don't see God making Adam and Eve as complete opposites. In fact, Eve was made out of Adam's very DNA. There are differences, for sure, but the differences complement instead of oppose.

As I said earlier, it is true that opposites can attract, *unless they don't.* Opposites may be cute at first, but real depth comes from shared values and commitments where a couple can say: "We are the same, we want the same, and we are in this together. It may be hard right now, but we can make it because we are *made for* one another."

Remember, you are looking for a *protagonist* in your story, not an *antagonist*!

Now, opposites can compliment like "he's a talker, and I'm a listener." But core values, worldview, soul priorities, and romance must match!

The title of this chapter and this point in particular may be one of the most important things you can learn from this book.

The person you are looking for should be "bone of your bones and flesh of your flesh."

You should think on the same wavelength and be committed to the same values. Please don't misunderstand; it does not mean that you have to have the exact same personality or backgrounds. It means that this person lines up with *you*!

2) We are three-part beings.

> *May God Himself, the God of peace, sanctify you through and through. May your whole **spirit, soul and body** be kept blameless at the coming of our Lord Jesus Christ.* **1 Thessalonians 5:23**

This seems pretty clear to me. If Paul was praying that their spirit and soul and body would all three be kept blameless, it means that they (and us) have three parts to our being.

One is called our body, the physical part of us.

The second is called our soul, the part of us that you cannot see but feel and interact with all the time. This is our "inner man" where we think and feel.

The third part of us is called our spirit, the part of us that interacts with God.

Some people believe that we are only two-part beings—that we have a physical part of us and an immaterial part of us. Now, whether or not you believe that we are two-part beings or three-part beings is really beside the point. The point is that we must find someone who is "bone of our bones" in the areas that matter most.

The main part of this principle is that we must line up in the *physical* and *intangible* aspects of our beings.

3) Perfect matches match us in the three parts of our beings.

Can two walk together, except they be agreed?
Amos 3:3 KJV

Here's where I may lose some of you, but Jon Courson's message hit me deeply at this point. Essentially, because we have three parts to our being, we should look for someone who matches us in *all three parts*!

Body: This is the physical part of us.

Some would be upset for me to say this, but I believe this is 100% true: *We are supposed to be romantically attracted to the person we marry!*

This is not to say that we should have unrealistic expectations or judge our future match based on looks. Not at all! Rather, we should be able to say that we have a romantic attraction to that person.

While there are many men and women who walk around solely judging based on looks, there are also people who are in danger of *settling* for someone that they agree with on worldview but have no attraction to romantically.

Now bear with me here. Beauty is in the eye of the beholder. So this, just like soul and spirit, is a *subjective* assessment.

My point in sharing this is to let you know that *it is completely normal to want to be attracted to your future spouse*. It is not arrogance or pride to desire a match in this way.

My wife was afraid that God would give her a guy that she was on the same page with for soul and spirit but not body! She thought it may be a test of humility to one day marry someone she found unattractive. She was afraid that it was *unspiritual* to desire attraction in a spouse, but she still prayed, hoping that God would give her a good looking man. (She says to tell you that He did.)

Soul: This is our inner man—the real us.

All that being said about attraction, we have been taught as a culture to find someone that we line up with physically while not caring about the other two parts of our being. We often overlook the realm of the soul.

The soul is a little harder to define than the body—mainly because our soul is an *intangible* part of us.

When we are cordial to people who are rude to us, but the real thought inside of us is, "I can't believe this guy is being so rude!"—*that* thought or feeling is the place of our soul. It is where our real thoughts reside on the inside.

Your soul is the seat of your affections, your emotions, and your thoughts. I like to call it, "the real you." When you go through your day, you can smile, wave, and say, "Sure thing, boss!" But when your head hits the pillow at night, the thoughts you think and the values you hold—that is the real you.

So it stands to reason that if you want to have a *genuine match*, you will *genuinely match* in the area of your soul. This is what is implied by the term "soul mates." It includes lining up in your worldview, values, and how you think.

Being with someone who thinks on a different wavelength is like living on opposite ends of the earth. No matter how hard you try, it is difficult to bridge the gap between each other because your souls do not line up.

We have another phrase in our culture that we use to describe what I'm saying. When we say that something "speaks to our souls," we are saying that it has touched us in a deep place. We *know* when something "speaks to our souls," but it is so hard to describe other than that we like it and want more of it. It leaves us feeling fulfilled or satisfied.

In fact, one of the ways we are progressively being sanctified or made holy is by learning to focus our energy and time on the things that we are called to, the things that speak to our soul. This could be everything from our life calling and passions to our everyday hobbies.

I know men who feel a deep calling to be out in nature but have dated women who hate it. This could be an issue later in marriage when the man wants to go for a week-long hiking trip and the wife wants to stay inside and read a book. These are obviously not deal-breakers but examples of how soul connection *does* matter!

Another example may be how someone relates to you. It may be cute at first when a guy is super inward and won't talk. But ten years from now, it will drive you nuts that he's not verbal and has no leadership skills whatsoever. These are things to consider *now* before you settle for someone who does not line up with you in the realm of your soul.

I am not saying that your perfect match has to like doing everything you do, but I am saying that the things that "speak to your soul" should line up.

When you line up in this area, you will not have constant arguments about how to spend your time, money, and resources.

Lining up in soul means that you will both be called to the same kinds of things. While you may each have your own avenues and tracks to run on, the nature of your calling and passions are the same.

Spirit: This is the part of us that relates to God.

While I listed this last, I believe it is the most important part of us that must match.

As Christians, we are not supposed to have a life partner who is not a believer.

> ***Do not be yoked together with unbelievers.*** *For what do righteousness and wickedness have in common? Or **what fellowship can light have with darkness?*** 2 Corinthians 6:14

But lining up in spirit means a lot more than meeting someone in a church service. It means that you share the same *depth* of intimacy and commitment to Jesus Christ. You are not trying to pull them up spiritually, and they are not your sole authority on spiritual matters. You both are able to go deep together spiritually. Seeking God in prayer, getting on your knees together, crying about the things that break God's heart—these are all shared values in the spiritual realm.

Imagine if you marry someone who is unequal in spiritual things. The way you approach a problem will be entirely different! Your spouse may want to sit and watch television while you want to pray for your sick child in the back bedroom. They may only want to go to church on Christmas and Easter, while you may want to be there all week serving. Look, these may seem like small examples, but can light and darkness mix together? According to the Bible—no way!

I cannot tell you how many couples I have met where one person wants to be *sold out* for God, but they feel held back because their partner still hasn't come around yet. This is the one regret I hear the most from people who wish they would've heard this teaching years ago. If you had to pick *only one* quality to line up in, I can guarantee you that you would want to line up in spirit.

Perfect Matches Not Perfect People

This is where we have to be careful with this concept. We are looking for the perfect *match*, not the perfect *person*.

If you have unrealistic expectations or want to part ways with someone simply because you don't line up on a few things, you'll never find the one.

When it comes to human beings, there are *no* perfect *people*. There are *no* perfect *relationships*. But there *are* perfect *matches*!

So it's important to note here that we are not talking about someone being right or wrong. This is not a conversation exclusively about having the same morals.

It is not *wrong* to have soul differences. We can acknowledge that someone is different from us without them being wrong. Recognizing these differences doesn't mean that you are good, and they are bad.

Ultimately, the things that need to line up will be between you and God. It is imperative that you start thinking about what is important in the *long-term* and not just the short-term.

In my previous relationship, I saw how we did not think on the same wavelength and share the same worldview. Our personalities were different, and the things that "spoke to my soul" did not speak to hers. This didn't make either of us wrong; it simply made us *different*.

You should evaluate whether you line up in these three parts of your being or not. Here are the mistakes people make in settling for *two* out of three instead of *three* out of three parts of our being.

Body And Soul

If you line up with someone in body and soul but not spirit, you will be romantically attracted to each other and love to do the same things.

You'll often think on the same wavelength—but your spiritual life will be dry as a rock! You'll feel like you live in the wilderness because your *true thirst* can only be quenched by God. To not share in spiritual things is not only sad but dangerous.

Most people who settle for this kind of relationship end up getting dragged down to the lowest common denominator of spirituality. That could mean a million things, but to make it simple, let me just say: *The likelihood of you bringing them up is way less than them dragging you down spiritually.*

Settling is a dangerous affair for your relationship with God!

Body And Spirit

This one is a little more unusual, but you could be romantically attracted to someone and both have a deeply personal walk with God but not share the same passions and calling on your life. You could have totally different personalities, worldviews, and desires.

To settle for two out of three here is a little more abstract, but there are plenty of spiritually deep people in the world whom you might be romantically attracted to but share nothing in common with in terms of soul priorities. You both could love God and find each other attractive, but you would be completely out of sync in the way you think, how you live, and what you pursue in life.

This could cause *many* disagreements and cause a couple to find *soul satisfaction* outside of their marriage. Trust me, if you cannot agree on issues that relate to your worldview, it can cause a lot of friction!

Soul And Spirit

Being deeply connected in soul things can endear you to someone romantically. So these are not cut-and-dry categories.

This combo means that you could be best buddies and love God but have no romantic attraction.

And remember, romantic attraction is not simply about how someone looks. There are so many examples from history about romance blossoming between people who once found each other repulsive. I'm even thinking of extreme examples where caretakers fell in love with disfigured service men from the war, etc.

So it's true that romantic attraction can develop over time. It is not based simply on first impressions. But, it also cannot be forced. One area of alignment (body, soul, or spirit) can eventually lead to another, but it's important that all three areas line up.

If you recognize that you truly do not have a romantic attraction to someone, that is a sign you shouldn't ignore! You are not a bad person to recognize this—you are saving yourself and them a lot of heartache later on. Just ask yourself if you feel like you are settling or trying to force an attraction that's not there.

Be Honest With Yourself

My personal plea to you is that if you are currently dating someone and know deep in your heart that you are settling, you would be honest with yourself. Don't settle for one or two out of three. Trust God to bring your *perfect* match.

Ask God if you have settled for someone other than your perfect match.

Don't try to get someone to change who they are. You cannot ask someone to try to change themselves just to fit you. It's not fair to them *or* to you.

The main idea here is that you would evaluate if someone matches the three core areas of your being. Obviously, we are not talking about perfection or agreeing on everything under the sun. But many Christian singles I meet are in danger of settling and compromising on areas that would negatively impact their unity in marriage.

So ask yourself the question: Am I considering lowering my standards just to be with *someone*?

Remember, Solomon said that it's better to be alone than with a nagging wife (Proverbs 25:24). So while being alone is "not good," we know that it's *still better* than being with the wrong person!

If you are single, consider yourself blessed to have learned about lining up with someone in the areas of body, soul, and spirit before committing to them in a deeper way.

May God Himself, the God of Peace, grant you the blessing of a perfect match—body, soul, and spirit!

07
How to Actually Break Up

Making The Choice

After realizing that I was dating someone who I did not line up with in all areas of body, soul, and spirit, I had a choice to make. Was I going to settle and stay together in spite of our different makeups, or was I going to end the relationship? I could not stay on the fence any longer.

I have already summarized the reasons why I was hesitant about breaking up. Once my suspicions about being with the wrong person were confirmed so powerfully by the teaching from the last chapter, I reached a crisis of decision.

The *finality of walking away* from a relationship is incredibly painful, but it is nothing in comparison with the *pain of staying* with the wrong person.

A book about finding the perfect match would not be complete without insight and instruction about how to properly move on from relationships where you are not with your match.

Remember that "failure" can be a good thing if it is aligning you with God's true desires for your life. Don't be afraid to follow God's leading to end a relationship—He always knows what is best for you!

<u>The Right Support System</u>

Aside from the fact that God is able to do anything, I am not sure I would've been able to end my relationship with Ashley apart from the friendship and support of three great men in my life: Luke, Barry, and Jason.

You've heard a lot about how my friend Luke was such a great support during this time. (And by the way, we ended up naming our second son Luke!) I'd like to share with you how my friends Barry and Jason were also instrumental as an example of how God sends the people you need to help you follow His plan for your life.

Jason was my small group leader at my college church where Christ got ahold of my life. He had a similar life story to mine and had already walked through the pain of ending a long relationship. At this point, I had been dating Ashley for about a year.

One day, Jason invited all of his small group members to attend a weekly Bible study where his friend Barry would be leading. I happened to have that lunch hour free in my college schedule, so I decided to try it out.

Barry was about 25 years my senior, and he would come to play a father figure role to me for years to come. One of the most life-changing teachings I heard during his Bible study was about having romantic relationships that honor God. Barry has an incredible wife, Kim, and he was happy to share how God sovereignly brought them together. His boldness about what a *God-honoring relationship* looked like helped me to long for my perfect match.

Inspired by Barry's wisdom, I continued to study God's design for relationships for the next year or so. I knew way back then the ramifications of what I was learning, but I was still far too insecure to break things off with Ashley. So I stayed with her longer and longer—further increasing the coming pain for both of us.

Over the course of that year, Jason and I became very close friends as he allowed me to process my situation without telling me what to do. I knew deep down, however, that it was all Jason could do to keep from telling me that I was with the *wrong person*. He trusted God to lead me to that decision, and I am grateful for how he gracefully counseled me and honored Ashley in the process.

When I First Tried To Break Up

After a while, I felt like I was not being genuinely committed to Ashley in my heart and that I had to be honest with her. This was about two years into our relationship, and I tried my best to end things then before our relationship developed further.

One night as I dropped her off at her apartment after hanging out, I decided to tell her how I truly felt. I didn't go into the conversation knowing that I was going to end it, but when the opportunity arose for me to be 100% honest, I finally confessed that I thought we should break up.

I knew in my heart that it was the right thing to do, but I felt *so insecure* that I didn't know if I could endure without going back to her. As I dropped her off, I explained that we could keep talking about this but that we should both get some rest and not talk more that night. I decided to make a detour on the drive back home. I went to the one person who I felt understood me and wanted the best for me—my friend Jason.

I could write a whole book about how Jason impacted my life, but suffice it to say, he had and still has my deepest respect. I called him around midnight. I was crying and asked him to get out of bed and talk to me in person. I only later realized how selfish it was for me to wake him up to counsel me in the middle of the night, but he graciously complied. He was so loving to come outside and talk in my truck by his house.

I told him that I had broken up with Ashley and that I didn't know if I could stick with it. I couldn't contain the emotion, and he literally held me while I cried. Since he had gone through his own painful breakup, he was totally able to identify with me about what I was going through. And he had a ton of discernment and wisdom to offer me which I lacked.

I only wish I had listened!

He told me that he was proud of me for doing what I thought was right even though it was so hard to do. Then he told me that he had one request. He asked me to promise him that I would not go back to her for at least one month. His suggestion was that I should take a whole month to clear my head and not be led by my emotions.

Being someone who wants to live with integrity, I did not make that promise. I knew there was a high probability that I would break it. So much of my life and identity was wrapped up in Ashley, and it was so hard to embrace this pain when I could have a "quick fix" of getting back together.

By the time I got home that night, it had only been a few hours, yet *the silence of being alone was deafening*!

Lacking Endurance

The next day Ashley showed up at my house early in the morning and in her pain told me that if she left I would never see her again. The finality of that ultimatum made me cringe inside, so I relented.

We decided to take a week apart and get re-grounded as well as see our campus pastor for some coaching.

When that week was up, we decided to get back together, and everything felt new again! We both had committed to changing things that weren't working, and it felt like this was the answer. The problem was that we were now operating out of insecurity because we knew that one misstep could totally end our relationship.

I am sure that I put a lot of pressure on Ashley which probably made her fear that I would break up with her again. I was living from a place of fear myself, so afraid that if I didn't keep an eye on things, they would go back to normal, and then I would be stuck.

The truth is, when it came to dating, we should've simply recognized our significant differences as evidence of our need to move on and not try to change one another.

So we stayed together for another whole year, and within that time, our attachment grew. So when we finally broke up a year later, *it felt like a death had occurred.*

<u>No Regrets</u>

I want to talk for a moment about regret. While it's clear now that God had a perfect match for me in someone else, it is important to note that I don't regret those years.

The Bible teaches that we have a salvation that leaves *no regret* (2 Corinthians 7:10). We can have godly sorrow, but not live in regret. It is critical to your destiny that you embrace the theology of *redemption.* God totally redeemed these years for me that many would say were wasted with the wrong person. *Redeemed* means that he made them fruitful and useful to my destiny. God took my missteps and turned them into stepping stones. He bridged the gap between my mistakes and my future.

God used that time to show me so many things, to develop my character, and to pave the way for what He had in store for me. Most of the things I learned were about my shortcomings and insecurities. He used the painful experiences of the past to peel back the layers and show me what was going on in my heart.

There have been several major decisions in my life where my wife and I leaned on the wisdom I gained during my time in those years and especially the final breakup.

I am so thankful that *the pain* I experienced in the past *is still bearing fruit* in my decisions today, reminding me about everything from avoiding complacency to ending things with integrity.

The Year Of Growth

God did not give up on me or my destiny, even when I made the choice to get back together with Ashley for another year. Over the course of that year, even while I was with the wrong person, I grew deeper in my walk with the LORD and my fellowship with the Christian men I have shared about.

The summer before my final year of college was a life-changing summer for me. I had a growing conviction in my heart that I was not supposed to stay in that relationship, but I needed to have 100% certainty about it.

God doesn't always show us things by writing it on the wall or sending an angel to tell us what to do. I would've even settled for one of my friends grabbing me and saying, "Dude! You are not supposed to be with her!" But none of those things happened.

What *did* happen was God kept confirming in various ways the reality that I knew deep down in my heart. Hearing the message about lining up in body, soul, and spirit was one of the crowning moments where I knew I needed to break up for good.

With that message in my heart and the wisdom from my past attempt at breaking up guiding me, I felt peace about ending my relationship with Ashley. Again, as I detailed in Chapter 1, it was probably the hardest thing I've ever had to do.

And to this day, I still praise God that He opened the door and carried me through!

How To Actually Break Up

For the rest of this chapter, I would like to share with you some of the things that I learned about how to *actually* break up with someone or end an engagement.

I use the word *actually* because I know all too well how hard it is to break up and stick with your decision. It takes confidence in the LORD and a desire to break up with integrity to not run back to that person when things get difficult. "Actually breaking up" means more than not getting back together, it means moving on.

These suggestions may be different for your personal situation and length of relationship, but they are principles that I wish I would've known the first time I tried to break up.

1) Prayerfully consider *if* you are supposed to break up.

You most likely don't have to rush things, unless God is telling you to end it today. What I mean is, in the same way that you will not want to be led by your emotions *to go back* to that person, you don't want to simply be led by your emotions *to leave* them.

This may seem obvious enough, but I know far too many couples who broke up in a heated argument yet never sought God about it. This left them on uncertain ground going forward, and many times they got back together. Without a conviction to move on for good, you highly increase the chance of reversing your decision later.

This decision is personal. You don't have to share with your significant other that you are processing this with God. Get away with the LORD and seek His leading for your next steps.

If you bring this up with your partner before you have made your decision, it really complicates your relationship. Then, the other person is compelled to operate from a defensive position and will usually do anything they can to keep you around. You don't need their advice on this matter. Besides, you already know that their advice will likely be: "Don't end it!"

2) Get counsel from someone who knows you well.

Don't go around airing your dirty laundry or gossiping about your partner, but do talk to someone you trust and let them know you are seeking wise counsel about if you should continue the relationship. Getting an outside perspective may help confirm what you sense God is showing you.

As I mentioned before, my friend Jason was instrumental in helping me process what God was showing me. He did not overstep his bounds, but he did share his personal experience which was what I needed in the moment.

While I didn't listen to Jason the first time, I really heeded his advice when the second and final breakup came around.

This was another way God redeemed the past—He taught me the incredible value of allowing someone to speak into my life. And this time, I listened!

3) Make the decision to break up or stay together.

If you feel that God is prompting you to end your relationship, do not sit on the fence forever. Eventually, not making a decision *is* making a decision. Complacency always makes terrible decisions.

I cannot tell you how dangerously close I was to getting engaged simply by not deciding. God was gracious, but I had to heed His clear directions to get off the fence. The easy route is to just stick with the status quo and avoid all friction, which is what many people choose to do.

So while you shouldn't rush into an emotional decision, you also shouldn't pretend like you have forever to figure this out. The longer you wait, the more attached you will probably become to one another.

Also, *do not* try to leverage a potential breakup for them to change. That's called manipulation, and it will place your relationship under bondage! I cannot tell you how wrong this is. Just don't do it!

4) Don't take a break, just break up!

Many people don't have a clear end to their relationship but decide to take a break for a while and see what happens. Often, the relationship just fizzles out from there.

Whether they realize it or not, people often choose to take a break so that they won't have to face the finality of a breakup. The fear of making the wrong decision can be paralyzing. To get around that, some choose to put the relationship on hold while they look for someone else. Then, if they cannot find someone they like better or if they realize they made a huge mistake, they have the option of restoring the previous relationship.

As appealing as it may be to your flesh to hang on to the person as a fallback, it is a cheap way to go about finding your match.

It does not give the other person the honor of clarity or the blessing to move on with their life.

The fear of making a mistake can keep you trapped in the wrong relationship. While it may seem relieving to not pull the trigger on a breakup, the real question is: *Do you trust that God's sovereignty is bigger than your mistakes?*

Believe in God's ability to lead you! If you doubt God's leading in your life, you'll operate from insecurity and hang on to what you know you should let go of.

5) Break up on purpose.

Don't wait to break up in the middle of an argument to prove your point. You should try to end things on good terms. It seems wise to talk to this person face to face and end things well.

Set aside a time. Don't pretend like everything is okay. Don't say you want to go on a date. You should be clear that there are some things you want to talk to them about.

If they ask if you are going to break up with them, I think you should do your best to be honest but try to wait to have the *full* conversation in person. You really want to be honoring and clear throughout the whole process. Don't tell them, "No way! Why would I do that?" That would only set them up for deeper hurt.

It is okay and reasonable for them to want to know what they are about to get into. You would want the same.

So saying something like, "I know this isn't the conversation you want to have, but I feel like we have to talk face to face about some hard things" is the right thing to do.

6) Honor them in the way you break up.

> Instead, **speaking the truth in love**, we will grow to become in every respect the mature body of Him who is the head, that is, Christ. **Ephesians 4:15**

This is a person that you probably have cared about for some time, so do not treat them like trash. It may make *you* feel better or more certain about your decision, but it's incredibly unloving. It is so important to honor them in the way you handle yourself, even if they don't treat you the same.

One of the most important things you can do in this breakup is to not go over the reasons why they "aren't good enough." You have made your decision, so there is no reason to try to change them now.

Instead of trying to justify your decision, you just need to be clear and stick with it.

If things start to escalate into an argument, ask the Holy Spirit to give you self-control. You should keep in mind during the conversation that this is a hard part of the process, but you will only make it harder by trying to prove them wrong.

No matter how much they may beg you to tell them all of their flaws, you must be resolved to not go out like this.

Perhaps by this point in time you believe that God has a perfect match for you and that this person isn't the one.

Praise God for that clarity! Cling to this, but don't use it as discussion material during the breakup.

You should not try to comfort them with the fact that there is someone else for them either. Many things may be true, but it doesn't mean you should say them. Sharing some things would be unloving or unkind.

You would think not saying these things would be social norms that everyone knows, but trust me, there are many well-meaning people out there who just spill the beans without respect for the individual to whom they are speaking.

7) Be considerate of their feelings, but don't be controlled by them.

Okay, I'm going to tell you straight up—this is a really hard line to walk. You want to err on the side of stoicism. It's not a good idea to get caught up in emotions—especially theirs.

At the same time, recognize that their emotions do matter in all of this. You must realize that you have had a lot more time to process this than they have. There should be the highest level of respect for the fact that this is inflicting fresh wounds in them.

You can let them know that you understand this is hard and that you don't want to hurt them.

While you want to be considerate of their feelings, you should not apologize. You may feel compassion for them because they are hurting, but you should not be sorry as if you have done something wrong. This is a decision that you have sought God about and can be confident in. So don't approach this as if you are doing something wrong.

There are many questions they may ask which could derail your discussion. Questions like, "So you don't love me anymore?" or "So everything we shared means nothing to you?" are not helpful in the moment, and you should identify them as such. Saying something along the lines of, "I'm not going to go down that road" is a nice way of saying that you will not be manipulated.

8) Don't blame *God* for your breakup.

One of the worst mistakes you could make is telling them that God told you to do this. Even if God has told you to do it, He hasn't told you to tell them that He told you! It is very insensitive to blame your breakup on God.

First of all, it makes them feel like you are superior to them in spiritual things. It's almost like telling them you heard from God and they didn't.

So as best as you can, it's good to stay away from mentioning that it's God's will for you to break up. Again, while that may be true, you don't have to say it.

9) Don't blame *them* for your breakup.

I mentioned this before, but it's worth reiterating as a principle. While it's true that some of their flaws may have led you to determine that they were not your match, the fact that they are not your match is ultimately not about their flaws at all. Even if they were perfect (which no one is), that still would not mean they are your match. That's why I've stressed so much that there are no perfect people. This is about lining up with another person.

There's no reason whatsoever to try and put the blame on them. Listing how they could've done better will only open the door to a discussion about giving them another chance.

As best as you can, you should avoid listing the reasons why they are not your match and keep your answers concise.

If someone has broken up with you before, you probably know it can be frustrating to *not* hear all of the reasons why they have chosen to move on, but the reality is that they are trying to honor you by ending on good terms.

It's a good idea to have a couple of the main reasons in mind why you don't line up and share those with them. If they keep pressing you for more details, you can repeat those things and say that you honestly think those are the main reasons that you need to share. Remember, don't be controlled by their emotions.

For example, my main reasons were that we didn't think on the same wavelength and had two different worldviews. I gave a few examples but tried to limit it to that. I know it was not everything that she wanted to hear, but I felt that it was the right response given the fact that I was committed to the decision I had made to end the relationship. By doing this, I felt that I was ending things in a way that honored her.

10) End the discussion.

At some point, it is self-defeating to continue the conversation. If they keep demanding answers that you either don't have or know you shouldn't give, there needs to be a point where you say the conversation should be done.

Be honoring in how you communicate, but at some point, tell them that you have made your decision and are sticking with it. It's important to be clear that *no amount of discussion* is going to change your decision.

It's best for both of you that this discussion should not linger on for hours or degrade into an out of control emotional argument.

11) End the relationship.

Wait, I thought we already broke up. Exactly. You cannot continue the relationship in the same manner after you have broken up.

It will be a great temptation to still talk on the phone and text each other, especially in your attempts to comfort them.

But you cannot be their emotional support during this time.

You may want to help, but remember, in their mind, it's *your* decision which is causing them pain. In their mind, if *you* would only change *your* decision, the pain would go away. So if you truly cared, they reason, then just change your decision and come back.

The nature of this situation is way more complicated than I could ever understand or explain. The best thing you can do is chose to progressively limit your communication with them.

These are not rules to follow. You are under God's grace. And I'm not suggesting that you cut them off immediately; but recognize that communicating the same way you always have will only keep the door open for getting back together. You have to be led by God about what that looks like, but I can tell you that after a day or two, I told Ashley that I didn't think it was a good idea for us to talk on the phone anymore. That may seem harsh or premature, but I knew that my tendency was to run back to the relationship. If I kept up communication the way it was, I knew that I would be betraying the conviction I felt as well as giving her false hope.

Now, please hear me out. You shouldn't operate out of fear, but you should use caution in your continued communications. To me, it seems harsh to cut them off the second you say, "We're done." But again, you cannot continue communication the same way as you always have.

Pray about a timeline, and follow God's leading even when it's hard.

The greatest temptation you will have is to be the support for them or try to stay close while still breaking up.

12) Delight yourself in the LORD.

> *Take delight in the LORD, and He will give you the desires of your heart.* **Psalm 37:4**

Lest we forget the main verse of this entire book, your focus at this time should be on your relationship with the LORD. This is a great time to learn what it means to lean on and fully depend upon Him.

After a breakup, it is a critical time for you to draw near to the LORD. He promises to draw near to you when you seek Him (James 4:8) and to be near to the brokenhearted (Psalm 34:18).

You should look at this as a time to heal and process your hurt with the LORD. He will comfort you in your pain and fill the insecurities that you may still have.

One of the best ways you can take delight in the LORD is by believing that He will not let you down.

Hold on to the promise that God has given you of a great future!

Use this time to grow in intimacy with God. Discover who He is to you. Invite Him to show you who He is as your Father and the pleasure He takes in you as His child (Mark 1:11). Learn to see Jesus as your Best Friend and Elder Brother

(John 15:15, Hebrews 2:11). Welcome the Holy Spirit to come to you as the Comforter (John 14:26, KJV).

The foundation that is laid with God during this time will be carried with you into marriage. Ask God show you that He is and always will be more than enough for you!

As I've tried to make crystal clear, marriage is not the answer to all of your problems—Jesus is.

13) Grieve your loss, but don't let nostalgia steal your destiny.

> *Forget the former things; do not dwell on the past. See, I am doing a new thing!* Now it springs up; do you not perceive it? I am making a way in the wilderness and streams in the wasteland. **Isaiah 43:18-19**

Breaking up feels like a death has occurred—and it has, the death of your relationship. Things will never be the same. Sometimes, that kind of finality can make us feel sad. It is okay to grieve the loss. You spent a lot of time with this person and made many memories. So take your hurt to God. Tell Him how you feel. And ask Him to give you peace that passes understanding (Philippians 4:6-7).

But don't let nostalgia creep in. At this point, you are very vulnerable, so let me be clear: *Nostalgia is an enemy to your destiny.*

If you find yourself reminiscing about the good times together, you are opening yourself up to emotions which are not in line with the revelation God has given you—that person was not the one!

That is why when I was given a box of mementos from Ashley, I originally decided I was going to throw it away. It would have been an unhealthy decision to hold on to those things.

I'm not saying to forget that person or pretend like they never existed, but dwelling on the past can make you miss the present things the LORD is doing in your life. Taking trips down memory lane or thinking back to the good times will only convolute the clarity you have had. Live in the truth that they were not God's perfect match for you.

Satan will only remind you of the good times with the wrong person. Why? Because one of his goals is trying to thwart our destinies. If you struggle with loneliness, you are more prone to the temptation of looking back and thinking, "At least I had *someone* then!"

14) Go forward!

> But one thing I do: **Forgetting what is behind** and **straining toward what is ahead,** I press on...**Philippians 3:13-14**

According to God's Word, we are supposed to forget what's behind and press forward to what Christ has for us.

Again, we are clearly told in the Bible to forget the former things—don't dwell on the past. But the reason *why* is because God wants to do a *new* thing.

He doesn't want us stuck in the past when He has a great plan and future for us. He is doing a new thing!

This doesn't mean that you should immediately start looking for the next relationship. In fact, after my breakup with Ashley, I felt led by God to take two months off from pursuing anyone at all. I mention that to you not as a model to follow but as a prayer to pray.

You should sincerely ask God if you are to take some time to regroup and heal before seeking a new relationship.

But that being said, don't put God in a box. This doesn't have to be a lonesome season for you. Don't assume that this is going to be a hard time for you. Remember, with God *all things* are possible (Matthew 19:26).

You still have a purpose now, even while you're waiting for your perfect match. So follow God's leading and don't grow complacent while you wait.

15) Stick with your decision.

I cannot drive this home enough. Had I done this the first time and taken Jason's advice to wait a month, I would not have spent another whole year in the wrong relationship.

I want to share something that happened which almost made me go back a second time. About an hour after we officially broke up for good, I was just coming home from a walk where I was processing things with God. Just as I got to my driveway, I got a phone call from Ashley. When I answered, I heard her crying on the other end. She told me she just found out terrible news, that her grandpa was diagnosed with terminal cancer. Talk about a terrible day.

Now the emotions of finality she was experiencing had to be incredibly amplified.

I remember lying on my driveway wondering, "How can I stay broken up with this girl?" I felt like it would be a terrible thing to stay broken up with her when she just found out such terrible news.

But my friend Jason helped me realize that being her support in this time would not be the loving thing to do. I would only be staying because I felt bad, not because I wanted to be with her. It would only kick the can down the road and cause more pain later on.

In other words, my emotional support wouldn't have been genuine. It would've portrayed a commitment to her that was no longer there.

To make matters worse, her grandpa died less than a week later. The temptation to be her support in this time was almost unbearable.

One of the biggest lessons I learned during this second and final break up was that emotional stability or stoicism in the moment is actually loving because it is not leading them on with false hope.

I'm not telling you to be cold, but please realize that your emotional stability in the moment may appear cold to them because they may want you to feel the sadness they feel. So be loving, but keep it together. I did my very best to honor her in this way.

Later, I bawled my eyes out. I kept praying for her. But by God's grace, I stuck with my decision.

If you start to doubt that God has a perfect match for you, it will be easy to go back on your decision. Stand firm and trust that God has not misled you!

> *Where there is no prophetic vision the people cast off restraint...* **Proverbs 29:18 ESV**

Without a vision people cast off restraint. This can mean that they "perish" or "grow strongly discouraged." So hold on to the vision God has given you and go forward. Don't give up or become discouraged.

Do not let fear keep you stuck. You can be confident that God is leading you and that He will not fail you!

Breaking Up With Integrity

A huge word of warning: *You cannot legitimately search for your perfect match while dating someone else.*

Think about it. Not only is it the wrong thing to do, it also sets you up to be dating a new person who was willing to get their foot in the door while you were taken! This at best speaks to immaturity and at worst speaks to a major character flaw. I'm so glad that the LORD finally brought me to a place of complete dependence upon Him so I could break up with Ashley, even while having no one else to go to.

Get Off The Fence

I love how author and speaker Kris Vallotton talks about the story of Abraham and Sarah from the Bible. One morning, God tells Abraham to get up and leave his family, his homeland, and his friends—everything that was familiar to him (Genesis 12:1). The Bible actually records that *Abraham didn't know where he was going* (Hebrews 11:8).

Kris Vallotton says, *"He only knew that he couldn't stay where he was."*[5]

Some of you are in a similar situation. You have no idea who or what God might have in store for you. You don't have any options in waiting, but you know that you cannot stay where you are.

I'd like to challenge you to get off the fence and step out in faith. *Your destiny is waiting.*

08
Clarify Your Criteria

One Powerful Question

That fateful day when my mom held me as I cried offered more than just a prophetic picture of my wedding day. It also offered tremendous insight into finding my perfect match.

After quite an emotional time, my mom and I sat there not saying much. Suddenly, she asked a powerful question which brought great clarity to my soul. She said, "Son, what do *you want* in a wife?"

As soon as I heard those words, it was as if a lightbulb turned on inside of me. That question revealed one of the fundamental errors I had made in pursuing relationships—*I had no criteria.*

I stumbled around trying to come up with an answer. I couldn't figure out what it was that I actually wanted in a wife.

Then I realized—I didn't know!

Let me explain. When I would be in a social setting and meet a girl, I would notice things about her that I liked. These were things like she's pretty, she's funny, she's into me, she laughs at my jokes. Those are not bad things, but they were always discovered *in that moment.*

The problem was that I would wait until I met someone to evaluate if they could be my match. Then, once I met them, I would make the person fit my non-existent criteria.

This left quite an open door for emotions to lead me instead of wisdom.

Being led by emotions can skew our vision. In fact, there were at least two girls in my past who I had told that I loved them. We spoke openly about getting married as if it was a foregone conclusion. I mention that just to show you how easily my emotions could carry me away from the blessing of wise decisions.

So if I was getting along with a girl I just met, I was always able to *find* things that I liked about her. But I had never in the quietness of singleness asked myself the question to know what I was looking for. In other words, what *kind* of person do I want as my wife? My tendency was to *find* things I liked rather than look for things that I *knew* I liked.

Knowing Before You Find

The reason why it is so important to know your criteria beforehand is so that you can objectively know the right person when you meet them. Sometimes we can get all caught up in emotions and find *good* things about a person but none of them are the *actual* things that will make your marriage great.

As you can imagine, this question immediately changed the way I approached finding my match. Immediately, I started writing out a list of things that I wanted in a spouse, and by the way, beauty was not on the list. (Although—like my wife's experience—I got that as a bonus as well!) This wasn't some chauvinistic compilation of shallow traits for a trophy wife. Far from it! I meticulously searched the scriptures and prayed about what kind of woman God wanted me to be with.

Biblical Guidance

Thanks to another pastor I listened to at the time, Bob Coy, I found such an amazing passage of scripture which helped me to clarify my criteria. He talked about how Proverbs 31 explains the kind of woman a man should be looking for.[6]

While we have already discussed how we should have a romantic attraction to our perfect match, look at what this passage reveals:

> *Charm is deceptive, and **beauty is fleeting; but a woman who fears the Lord** is to be praised.* **Proverbs 31:30**

A woman who fears the LORD! *That's* what I was after!

I finally knew *who* I was looking for.

I could easily be attracted to a whole host of women who were beautiful on the outside but did not fear the LORD. That was not the kind of depth that I wanted in a wife.

Immediately I thought of the girls I knew who had flirted with me but to my knowledge were not women who had a relationship with the LORD. I knew it would be a temptation for me to find validation with them, so I avoided them like the plague! You may think that was not very kind of me, but the reality is that I was in a very vulnerable place and knew my past tendencies of falling for the person who showed any interest in me at all. I wanted to carefully guard the gift the LORD had given me of a fresh start to find the one I was made for!

To that end, I knew more than ever that the most important thing I could do was guard myself from the wrong relationship.

This required a purity of heart and an unwavering commitment to the conviction God had given me.

Don't Get Burned

What I'm telling you is to not go randomly looking for matches or you might get burned! You must know in your heart the kind of person you are looking for so that you'll know when you actually meet them.

So many people walk with a poverty mentality: "I guess I should just be happy that *somebody* wants me." And they lower their standards.

You shouldn't have *unrealistic* expectations, but you should *have* expectations if you value yourself and know your worth. Writing them down is not prideful, it's prudent—you've got to have the integrity to know yourself and learn from the past.

While it's true that prideful people with unrealistic expectations won't find anyone who's "good enough," I have met far more singles who are in danger of settling. This would be to their own detriment. So don't be stuck up, but also don't be like I was—"tossed to and fro by the waves" (Ephesians 4:14).

Pray about it. Search the scriptures for the kind of person God wants you to be with. Don't start with a list of people, start with a list of criteria.

My List

I have debated about whether or not to share with you my personal criteria for the woman I was looking for. After prayerful consideration, I've decided not to include it here for several reasons.

Mainly, I don't want people to simply adopt it as their own. Everyone should take the time to get alone with God and search the scriptures for themselves.

Many of the things on my list were things that are wise to have in a spouse, but many were simply preferences. Some had to do with my own personality and passions, while others had to do with my beliefs and worldview. It is hard to simply list criteria without being able to explain how I felt led to each one.

Since I don't have the space to do that here, I have decided to make it available to you online. My wife and I have prepared a full E-Course curriculum called "Finding the One" to help you discover your match. You can access the E-Course (including my personal criteria list) at *perfectmatchcoaching.com*.

In one of the lessons, we help you develop your own criteria list, and I walk you through my own list that I made years ago.

If you are interested in going deeper than the pages of this book allow and preparing for your match, I suggest you go there.

A huge bonus to the E-Course is that everyone who takes the course gets my eBook, *7 Signs that God has Someone for You*, completely free. That's 100% exclusive content that doesn't show up in this book. In one of the lessons of the E-Course, my wife and I walk you through the process of discerning if God has someone for you. We give specific examples of ways that God may be confirming to you that your waiting is not in vain!

If you plan to enroll in the E-Course, don't forget to use the coupon at the back of this book for half off!

However, for the purposes of this writing, my hope is that you will decide to seek God for yourself on what *kind* of spouse He wants you to find.

I did not go around interviewing potential partners or find out if they matched all of my criteria right away. It takes time to get to know someone to see whether or not they are the one you have prayed for.

Clarifying your criteria will allow you to have discernment about if someone could be the one you have been waiting for.

Amazingly, as I got to know my future wife Korie, she met *all* of my criteria. From then on, I have never had a doubt that she was the one for me, even when hard times came—and they did.

Establishing criteria allowed me to walk with confidence and to know that I was not settling.

Don't Settle

If you don't have criteria in mind, you are way more likely to be led by your emotions and settle for less than God's best.

Be led by His wisdom and not simply by how you feel in the moment.

This is my personal plea to you to not try to stretch how someone could be a fit but to honestly evaluate whether a relationship with them would be choosing to settle.

The Most Important Thing

As you have seen already, lining up spiritually is one of the most critical parts of finding your match. Honestly, while so many things may be personal preferences, this one is not.

Have you ever thought someone would be the perfect match if they would only believe in God? I have. You think, "I'll start dating them and be a light in their life. Eventually, they'll come around and become a Christian." In the Christian world, we call this "Missionary Dating." That is a pejorative term, by the way, to describe something that is almost designed to fail.

God's Word is clear that if you are a believer in Jesus, you should not marry an unbeliever.

> *Do not be yoked together with unbelievers. For what do righteousness and wickedness have in common? Or what fellowship can light have with darkness?* **2 Corinthians 6:14**

Do not even entertain the idea of dating a non-believer. I would also suggest to you that if they are not pursuing Christ at the same level you are, they will only bring you down. Suffice it to say, the person with the lowest maturity level usually ends up being the high-water mark for your collective walk with Christ.

Why would you be willing to compromise in what you claim is the most important area of your life?

Let's say this person does come around and says they are a believer. Can you be certain that they aren't doing that just so you will marry them? Also, if they have no depth of relationship with Christ and you start dating them, almost every experience I've seen says that it will pull you down to their level, not the other way around.

Don't try to be some spiritual superhero like you are going to rescue them with your superpowers of dating. You are signing up for a world of hurt.

Again, I'm not saying this has never happened, but as you have hopefully learned in this book, the exceptions are never the rule!

Don't sacrifice your relationship with the LORD on the altar of idolatry for a spouse.

The Real Perfect Match

This is a perfect time to tell you about how the bigger picture of our lives isn't about who we will marry on earth but our eternal marriage to Jesus Christ.

This may be a strange concept to embrace (especially for men), but the Biblical reality is that in heaven, we will forever be rejoicing in our relationship with Him!

> *When the dead rise, **they will neither marry nor be given in marriage**; they will be like the angels in heaven.* **Mark 12:25**

In response to some people who were trying to trip up Jesus with their inferential theology, Jesus puts marriage in proper perspective. The tricksters were asking that if a woman was married and widowed seven times to seven different brothers (an extremely hypothetical situation—*also called an exception*), who gets to be married to her in heaven?

Jesus gives an incredible answer: *Your perfect match on earth won't be your Perfect Match in heaven.*

Jesus reveals the importance of seeing Him as the Perfect Husband. While we will certainly know and love and celebrate together with our loved ones who are in heaven, we will not be given in marriage as we are on earth.

The marriage feast of the Lamb will be in full effect (Revelation 19:9), and we will forever be caught up in our intimacy with Him.

So don't make marriage an idol!

Make Jesus your number one desire, and enjoy all of the good things—including marriage—that He gives you here on earth.

09
Preparing for Your Match

Don't Wait—Start Today!

This is one of the most exciting chapters to share because it is all about things you can do *right now* to prepare for your perfect match.

Believing that God is the one who will bring your match can have an unintended negative consequence of feeling helpless or in limbo until God moves. But that's not true!

The reality is, we can participate with Him as He prepares us, and we can operate with wisdom to guard ourselves against doing something to disrupt His plan or dishonor our future spouse.

Am I That Person?

Andy Stanley, the pastor of Atlanta-based North Point Ministries, sums up the power of our present choices to impact our future relationships by posing a powerful question: *"Are you who the person you are looking for is looking for?"*[7]

Another way of saying it is, am I more focused on *finding* the right person or *becoming* the right person? This helps us to stay moldable while God shapes us for our perfect match.

Many Christians want a man or woman who is "all-in" for the LORD even when they themselves are not!

So ask yourself: "Am I developing the kind of character that will attract someone like that?"

"Does my devotion to the LORD match the level I want in my future spouse?"

"Would someone with the caliber I am looking for be looking for someone with the caliber I possess?"

Start paying attention to the kind of person you *need to be* for the kind of person you *want to be with*.

Honoring The Past, Honoring The Future

Now all that being said, let me share with you a theology that has the power to greatly affect your future by preparing for your future match *today*.

If you read the story of Ruth, a young widow in the Bible, you'll read about how her husband dies and she chooses to leave her culture and chances of finding another husband to follow her mother-in-law Naomi.

She decides to honor Naomi by going with her and leaving her homeland—which is tantamount to choosing to be a widow for life. And if you've read it before, you know that things end very well for Ruth who gets to marry the man of her dreams—wealthy, handsome, and wise Boaz. (The only thing that's not attractive about him is his name!)

There is so much that happens in this story, but I want you to see what was going on behind the scenes as she made this life-changing decision.

Ruth makes a decision in her present to honor the past.

> *Then Naomi said to her two daughters-in-law, "Go back, each of you, to your mother's home. May the LORD show you kindness, **as you have shown kindness to your dead** husbands and to me."*
> **Ruth 1:8**

I think that's a strange way for Naomi to describe their kindness. She says that the sisters are not just showing honor to Naomi but also to their husbands. It was as if the way they handled themselves *after* their husbands passed away would have been pleasing in their eyes. This honored their dead husbands!

And I want you to think about something: *If we can honor people from the past, could it be true that we can honor people from the future?*

That may sound strange, but the Bible shares very clearly that we can!

Their Shoes

> *She does him good, and not harm, **all the days** of her life.* **Proverbs 31:12 ESV**

Are you are committed to doing your spouse good *all* the days of your life? Including the days *before* you have even met?

One of the most powerful things you will choose to do while you prepare for your future match is to make decisions in light of what will honor them.

This will require sacrifices that are often inconvenient but truly an act of faith. And faith is one of the requirements to inherit promises, as you will see next chapter.

Faith requires you to do something now that may not make sense in your *current* context but makes a ton of sense for your *future* reality.

Make your decisions in a way which will do good to your future spouse now. You must start to look at things from their perspective.

Many of the things I am going to suggest to you in this chapter do not make sense unless you put yourself in their shoes. What would you want?

How would you want yourself to behave if you were them?

How do you hope *they* are conducting themselves now?

In light of those answers, what choices do you need to make *now* to honor them—perhaps before you've even met?

We are supposed to give honor where honor is due (Romans 13:7). Since you know that God has an *amazing* match for you, you can be sure that they *are* due honor. So go ahead and honor them now. This perspective is an amazing way to walk by faith that God has a perfect match for you!

Walking By Faith

So how do you honor your future spouse? You honor them now by living like they actually exist and that God's promise is true. It's that simple.

We call that walking by faith and not by sight (2 Corinthians 5:7). It means doing things in accordance with what you believe but cannot yet see.

So here are eight suggestions that I strongly encourage you to employ to honor your future spouse and pave the way for the day you meet your match!

1) **Pray for them.**

This may seem obvious, but in all of your dreaming about a perfect match, it can be easy to forget that they are alive *right now*! They need your prayers.

Don't just pray to *find* them. Pray *for* them. Pray for God to prepare them. Pray for God to bless them and draw them near to Him.

My wife was praying for me long before I was someone she would've wanted to be with. We often joke that if we had met in high school or even at the start of my college career, we wouldn't be together today. That is because I was a totally different person then. But she was praying for God to *intervene* in my life and to help me be the man He was calling me to be.

While I don't understand all the ways prayer works, it is a humbling thing to realize that some of Korie's prayers could have helped me become the *kind* of man she was looking for!

It could've been some of these very prayers that helped me move from a place of complacency to conviction—not only ending my former relationship but drawing closer to God more than ever before.

Also, *now* is never too early to begin praying for your future relationship together. You never know when you will meet your perfect match, and you will want your relationship to be covered in prayer from the start. So pray for them to be the person God is calling them to be today *and* in the future.

I felt led to start praying in faith for my future spouse once I found out what kind of person I was seeking. This is exactly what my future wife was doing for me at the time!

I wanted God to move in her life, draw her close, and teach her how to delight in Him. While I didn't know where she was at the time, I knew from experience that as a single longing for companionship, the temptation to walk outside of God's will was strong.

I knew that if I needed prayer, she probably did too!

Here is a prayer I recorded in my journal years ago as I was seeking God for His perfect match for me:

> *"God please provide for me Your daughter, a Christian woman, as my wife. Please send me a woman who fears Your Name more than she does me. Please God, I implore You, bring about a wife for me whose identity is in You alone and not caught up in me. Give me the wisdom to discern the difference and to see Your knocking—to not slam doors at opportunities or signs. God, give me a discerning heart that is able to recognize a woman who fears Your Name alone. Do not let me be unequally yoked, but throw off my chains and bondage to the lies of Satan which cause me to fear. Instead, produce in me a joy that is bursting forth in my heart from the hope of Your plans. Help me to wait on You and Your promise, and please continue a good work in me, fanning the fire in my heart by Your Holy Spirit."*

2) Interact with others as if your future spouse is already secured.

When God brings this person along in your life, you will not have to force it to happen. You should be able to handle your social life with confidence in light of the fact that your future is *secure*.

It may be easy while you're single to be super friendly with everyone you meet, but it is never too early to learn how to properly relate to others in a way that honors your spouse!

This means that if you are a woman interacting with men, you do it in a way that keeps your future husband in mind. I'm not saying he couldn't be one of those people, but if you are someone who is prone to flirt with every potential suitor you meet, that is not an honoring thing to your future spouse. If you are a man interacting with women, are you doing it in a way that keeps your future wife in mind? You can love, honor, and cherish her *before you ever meet* by the way you interact with *other* women.

3) Keep your heart for your future spouse.

On our honeymoon, Korie gave me a very special gift that she had been making for me since before we ever met.

Many years beforehand, Korie began keeping a journal to her future spouse. She would write about things that were going on in her life, the hardships of waiting, and the joys of the future she was hoping for. This was a way for her to not only honor me but also to keep her perspective that she was waiting for someone very special.

It kept her focus on God's promise to her, and it allowed her to have wisdom in the moment while waiting for a future that sometimes felt uncertain. Sometimes her journal entries were brutally honest about how hard it was or the doubts she may be feeling about if God had a husband for her. Other times she wrote prayers to God asking for strength while she waited. She even included some apologies for when she gave pieces of her heart away or found emotional fulfillment in other men.

That was one of the most precious gifts anyone has ever given me. Not simply the journal, but the purposeful attempt of keeping her heart pure and staying committed to me long before we ever met. That was a gift she decided to purchase for me years before we first laid eyes on one another.

This is another way to walk by faith and honor your future spouse. It doesn't have to be a journal, but can you think of a way to show your spouse how you were saving yourself for them from before you ever met?

This brings me to some harder choices you may have to make.

4) Don't stay close with past flames.

This one may be harder to hear, and I know you may have reasons why your situation could be different. Again, we are not focusing on exceptions here but on the big picture. And *in general*, it is not wise to try to stay friends with your exes.

I am not saying that you should pretend like they no longer exist. But this point needs to resonate with you: *Keeping your past too close may keep your future far away.*

In other words, the way you handle your post-relationship with your ex has a great potential to affect your future relationship.

If you are going to honor your future spouse, you need to have in mind what would be "doing good" (Proverbs 31:12, ESV) to them now. This is one of the things that will help you start out on solid ground when your match comes along. For them to know that you have completely moved on from past flames will reassure them that you are a person they can trust and fully commit to.

Really, no woman wants to start dating a guy who is still spending time with his ex-girlfriend—and vice versa. It's not that they should just trust you more; it's that if you are still holding on to that relationship, there's no guarantee to your new partner that you have fully moved on. What girl wants a guy who is still emotionally connected to another woman?

It is very tempting to stay close to an ex because it temporarily eases the pain and lessens the feelings of finality, but blurring the lines with your past will only complicate your future.

If this one is hard for you to accept, then the next choice will be even harder...

5) Don't let your primary friendships be with the opposite sex.

Okay, I may tick some people off right here. First of all, I'm not saying you cannot engage socially with the opposite sex. If that were the case, then I wouldn't have gotten to know my wife Korie because we started as friends.

I'm also not saying that it's *wrong* to have friends of the opposite sex. I am saying that it's not wise to let them be your *primary* friendships.

The Bible says that men grow and are sharpened by close community with other men (Proverbs 27:17). I have already shared about how having close male friends in my life was part of God's plan for helping me discover my destiny. I know for my wife Korie, the many women who poured into her over the years helped her become the God-fearing woman that she is today. *They helped her fall in love with Jesus long before she ever fell in love with me.*

Something is lost when men aren't sharpening men or women are no longer sharpening other women. I think the breakdown of deep, mentoring relationships with the same gender has caused a lot of dysfunction in our society.

There is something powerful about having friendships where we can share brotherly and sisterly love and also smooth out the rough places in our lives. There is so much potential for growth as we seek to glorify God together through friendship.

But when it comes to having deeply personal relationships with the *opposite* gender, my caution is due not only to the *complexity* but also to the *consequences*.

Many times, people who have friends of the opposite sex are able to get some of the same emotional fulfillment that they would from a romantic relationship but without the commitment. You are able to give a precious part of yourself away—even if it's not physical—that should be saved for your spouse.

Perhaps some of this is due to people not wanting to commit. "Defining the relationship" has become a forced conversation when one friend may have "read into" things more than they should have.

Countless singles have been hurt by someone who inadvertently led them on—only later to claim that they would never have wanted to imply something more than friendship. *They* don't see how you could've misunderstood their intentions.

But I see how—because deep friendships with the opposite sex can develop intimacy that is best saved for romantic relationships.

It may be fun. It may feel free. But without commitment, there is a tendency to enjoy some of the benefits of a romantic relationship while still calling it a friendship.

Walking with integrity now will set you up for a lifetime of trust later. Many of the problems I have witnessed as I counseled couples approaching marriage has been about one of the partners having lots of friends of the opposite sex.

I have even counseled a couple where *both* of them had primary friendships of the opposite sex, and they *both* wanted *the other person* to stop seeing those friends, but *neither* would relent!

Getting deeply close with the opposite sex is like giving something away that belongs to your future spouse. No, I'm not putting this on the same level with cheating, but I truly don't feel that it is an honoring thing to do.

And for those that say it's completely platonic, that's fine, but what will your future spouse think about all those guy or girl friends?

Again, I cannot tell you how many people my wife and I have counseled where this becomes a problem. When you are single, it may not seem like an issue. But the second you have a significant other, this can become a roadblock. Many people are then faced with the question of continuing to have these friendships or pursuing an exclusive romantic relationship.

My wife has shared about the men in high school and college who surrounded themselves with women as their primary friendships. She said they may have been nice people, but they were never contenders to be her husband. She was turned off by it because those men were gaining emotional security from those relationships.

Put yourself in your future spouse's shoes.

Will they be happy for you to spend most of your time with the opposite sex? Are you going to be getting counsel and having intimate conversations with these friends once you are married? When you want to have a night out with friends, will you tell your husband or wife that you are going to go to a movie with someone of the opposite sex?

Please don't make the mistake of thinking that having primary friendships of the opposite sex is the mature thing to do. Honestly, I cannot tell you how many issues this has caused among friends of mine. And there were also a couple instances where it broke trust in relationships.

Don't poison your future relationship by having unhealthy friendships with the opposite sex.

The problem relationships that I have counseled were often ones where the woman was unable to get along with other women, and the man either had no male friends or surrounded himself with a few close women friendships.

You may think that if they really value you, they will be fine with you having these friendships. Isn't that like saying that if you can't have these friends you would rather be single? I don't care who you are; most women do not want their husband running around with other women—and most men do not want their wife running around with other men.

One of the best ways you can honor your future spouse is by not finding emotional fulfillment in the opposite sex. Save that for your perfect match.

I'm not saying that you should end all of your friendships— but you *must* be discerning! Keeping your future spouse in mind is the way to discern if you are conducting these friendships in a way that dishonors them.

6) Write down your criteria and study it.

You don't have to get over-the-top here, but it would be a wise choice to not only have a list of criteria but also write it down and study it. Don't just have it in your head. Emotions will always try to stretch your criteria or blur the lines to fit the person. It's great to be super familiar with the kind of person you are looking for *before* you start looking.

One thing I began doing in this time was memorizing Proverbs 31 so that I had ingrained in me the kind of woman I was waiting for—someone special.

I still remember spending time with Korie, and verses from Proverbs 31 would come to mind as she would talk. "She opens her mouth with wisdom, and the teaching of kindness is on her tongue" (Proverbs 31:26, ESV). It was like the LORD was confirming to me point by point that this woman was my perfect match. But I was able to recognize this because I had prayerfully predetermined and meditated on Biblical criteria.

7) Commit to purity before you ever meet the person.

When things start to progress romantically with someone, it is imperative that you have already established boundaries in your mind beforehand.

When Korie and I started dating, she told me that she didn't want to kiss a guy until she was *engaged*. (Jaw drop!) Far from turning me off, it made me see how valuable she was! It made me further committed to protecting her purity.

By the way, my wife and I both believe that these are *personal* areas of conviction that you must work out with the LORD. We don't think it's wrong to kiss before engagement or something like that, but for *our* relationship (and based on my insecurities at the time) it was wise for us to set clear boundaries.

There's no guarantee that the next person you decide to go on a date with is your perfect match. So from the start, be committed to taking it slow—even if this person meets all of your criteria.

A great question to ask yourself is, "Will the way I am relating to someone *now* be honoring to my future spouse if *this person* ends up not being *that person*?"

Here is something that needs to be at the forefront of your thinking if you meet a potential match: *You are not married yet.*

No matter how great this person may be or how your dating relationship may progress, don't pretend to be married if you are not. This is one of the most important things to remember if you are committed to honoring your future spouse. Even if you *think* this person is your future spouse, they *are not* your spouse *yet*.

I have watched couples who were sold out for the LORD throw away their purity simply because they thought they were going to marry that person anyway. But they were not married yet!

This is a popular lie of the enemy, and I know from my own past that Satan is good at getting you to let your guard down because you think you have found the one! This causes all kinds of trouble.

As I mentioned earlier, there were at least two girls that I dated where we casually discussed wedding plans like it was a foregone conclusion that we would get married!

Acting like you are married when you are not, even in conversation, can be a slippery slope. If you are dating someone that you think is the "one," you could easily let go of boundaries that you once held as sacred.

So when Korie and I started dating, we expressly agreed to three things.

1) Marriage talk was off the table. We actually committed to *not* talking about future stuff but to enjoy the present and get to know one another. We believed that God would make clear in *His* timing any next steps we needed to take.

2) Failure *was* an option. From the start, we refused to embrace the pressure of "making it work." We both said that if we were not a fit we would not continue the relationship, and that would be okay. We would not let the fear of failure keep us locked in!

3) Purity was our priority. I already mentioned how Korie didn't want to kiss until she was engaged. But we agreed to keep each other accountable for not pushing boundaries. Being open about our commitment to walk in purity was critical to us not being deceived by the enemy's crafty lies— especially his famous lie, "You're going to get married anyway, so why wait?"

Please don't buy the lie of the enemy. The treasure of your purity is something to guard even when you are single.

It's important to have a good foundation and total commitment to purity *before* you enter a possible lifelong relationship. This starts with your individual purity.

> *But among you **there must not be even a hint** of sexual immorality, or of any kind of impurity, or of greed, because these are improper for God's holy people.* **Ephesians 5:3**

While we don't have to be perfect before God will bring us our match, it stands to reason that just like any good parent, He wouldn't want to give you His precious daughter or son if you are living in impurity.

For example, I cannot begin to tell you how many relationships I have seen damaged by one person's addiction to pornography.

These were addictions that started before a relationship ever began, and as we have discussed, were not cured simply by being with someone.

8) Spend time with godly married couples.

If experience is a great teacher, then you want to be taught by the failures and successes of those who have gone before you.

It would be awesome if you don't have to go through the same hardships that they did and yet still learn what they have learned. Being exposed to other marriages will help you start seeing your own strengths and weaknesses which you might have unknowingly learned from your family growing up.

Spending time with happily married couples will give you a vision for the future and keep the embers of promise burning in your heart. It will teach you to rejoice with those who rejoice (Romans 12:15) and not become bitter about people who have found their perfect match before you have.

9) Keep living your life.

I have met many singles who seemed to literally put their lives on hold until God brought their match. This is a bad idea on many levels—namely because as we've seen in both the Bible and real life, it is within the context of normal living that *many* people meet their future spouse!

Even in the Biblical account of Ruth as we saw earlier, it was in the context of her normal daily responsibilities that God brought about her perfect match, Boaz. She worked hard in the fields every day just to bring home food for herself and her mother-in-law, and it was in that *normal* environment that her life was forever changed! Don't try to map out scenarios of how it could all go down—just keep living your life!

Also, as much as you may hate to hear it, there are many upsides to this season of your life. There is a long list of perks to being single like being able to be spontaneous, go on trips, or have overnight events with your friends. Live it up!

Your money is currently yours. While you want to honor your future spouse with how you handle your finances, you have flexibility now that you may not in the future. So go on ice cream dates with friends or out to a movie and enjoy the freedom that having no attachments has to offer.

I remember when I was first single after my breakup, I was able to stay by the side of my friend, Merv, in the days leading up to his wife passing away from cancer. I remember being at the nursing home at about three in the morning praying with them and realizing how free I felt knowing that I didn't have to text anyone or let anyone in the world know where I was!

10) Invest in spiritual things.

> For **where your treasure is,** there your heart will be also. **Matthew 6:21**

Since you will want to be in your clearest frame of mind to make major decisions when a potential match comes along, it is a wise decision to pursue spiritual things like never before.

Get involved in a church small group. Find some brothers or sisters in Christ who you can mature with. Talk to God regularly. Spend time in His Word. Read books about becoming the man or woman God desires you to be. (This book was a good start!)

Surrounding yourself with the right community will open up the opportunity to receive counsel from trusted believers when the time comes. When I thought Korie was the one I was supposed to pursue, I was *very* careful about not rushing in too quickly or making the wrong decision.

I wrote out questions in notebooks and interviewed several close mentors as well as mutual friends between Korie and I. I asked them questions about if they thought I was healed from my past and ready to date again. I asked them questions about Korie and if they thought she was ready for a relationship. I even met Korie's parents and asked them the same questions as well as getting their permission to date her.

These were things I was able to do because I was spiritually grounded and had a community of believers around me who supported me. The time between breaking up and starting to date another person was one of the most intense (in a good way) seasons of personal growth and intimacy with the LORD I have ever had.

If you want to go deeper, I strongly suggest you take advantage of our half-off coupon in the back of the book for our E-Course, "Finding the One." It is 12 lessons divided into 6 weeks—all about stepping into your 1 destiny.

Or, if you desire personal coaching with Korie and I, we'd be happy to set up an appointment with you at perfectmatchcoaching.com.

So invest in spiritual things like never before. It will be time well spent. Time spent with God is never wasted! After all, *He is incredibly able* to bring His promises to pass. Which is what the rest of this book is all about...

Part III: The Fulfillment

10
Inheriting Promises

And so, after he had patiently endured, **he obtained the promise. Hebrews 6:15 KJV**

"Abraham was long tried, but he was richly rewarded. The Lord tried him by delaying to fulfill His promise. Satan tried him by temptation; men tried him by jealousy, distrust, and opposition; Sarah tried him by her peevishness. But he patiently endured. He did not question God's veracity, nor limit His power, nor doubt His faithfulness, nor grieve His love; but he bowed to Divine Sovereignty, submitted to Infinite Wisdom, and was silent under delays, waiting the Lord's time. And so, having patiently endured, he obtained the promise.

God's promises cannot fail of their accomplishment. Patient waiters cannot be disappointed. Believing expectation shall be realized. Beloved, Abraham's conduct condemns a hasty spirit, reproves a murmuring one, commends a patient one, and encourages quiet submission to God's will and way.

Remember, Abraham was tried; he patiently waited; he received the promise, and was satisfied. Imitate his example, and you will share the same blessing."

-Excerpt from *Streams in the Desert*, L.B. Cowman[8]

It Will Happen!

The purpose of this chapter is simple—to encourage you that God *will do* what He has promised. If you are unsure about God's promises to you, I encourage you to study scripture and pray and ask Him about His plans to bring you a spouse.

Also, I have written an eBook called *7 Signs that God has Someone for You*. This has exclusive content about discerning if God is promising you a spouse. Again, you can get the eBook free when you enroll in our E-Course, "Finding the One" at perfectmatchcoaching.com. Or, you can purchase it separately on Amazon if you desire.

Additionally, as we have talked about already, don't ignore your desires. Often, that desire is God's way of showing you in advance what He will bring you in the future (like showing Adam his need in the garden and then fulfilling it).

This is the amazing reality of our God: He *will* bring to pass the promises He has made! One day, it's going to happen for you. This entire book has been about preparing you for that kind of prophetic fulfillment.

God is faithful to do what He says He will do. We can take His promises to the bank. But the Bible says that we don't *earn* promises; we *inherit* them.

This means that you cannot *force* your destiny into existence —you can only place yourself in the right posture to *receive* it.

The Missing Ingredient

*We do not want you to become lazy, but to imitate those who through **faith and patience inherit** what has been promised.* **Hebrews 6:12**

I was taught for my entire Christian experience that the key to victory in our lives is faith—that everything hinged on whether or not we would believe God and take Him at His word.

I was brought up in a church that talked about "faith alone" as the way to receive salvation. I believe what the Bible says —that we are saved through faith (Ephesians 2:8-9).

I am glad that I was not raised under a theology of trying to work for or earn God's love and acceptance. I am so grateful for a generally accepted teaching among believers that we should live our lives by faith in God in everything we do.

It was clear to me from a young age that our salvation and going to heaven when we die has nothing to do with how good or bad we are but has everything to do with believing in Jesus and what He has already done for us on the cross.

But what I was *not* taught over those years was that faith isn't just what we believe in our heads but also the *posture* of our hearts.

When it comes to seeing your promise come to pass, there is a different aspect of faith that is often overlooked. The Bible says you must have faith *and patience* (Hebrews 6:12).

It is one thing to believe that God will do what He has said; it's quite another to wait for Him with the right heart.

The heart posture of patience is the avenue of inheritance.

In other words, patience is waiting in faith for God to bring His promises to pass. Faith waits with *patience*.

In our day, patience seems to be watered down to being able to wait in line at the grocery store or at a stop light without getting upset. And while that may be good practice, patience actually has everything to do with *how you wait* for your destiny.

So if you believe that you are waiting on God to bring about His promise, ask yourself this question: Am I waiting with patience? Sometimes, we think we are waiting on God, but He may be waiting on us to wait on Him with the right heart.

He Sat Down

Let me put it to you this way.

> But when Christ had offered for all time a single sacrifice for sins, **He sat down** at the right hand of God, **waiting** from that time until His enemies should be made a footstool for His feet.
> **Hebrews 10:12-13 ESV**

When Jesus offered up His life as a sacrifice for our sins, He had complete and total victory. And what did He do next?

He sat down.

Those three words summarize so much about our Christian life. Ours is the walk of faith, and the position of victory is *seated.*

Seated is a heart posture of rest and trust in the LORD. From this place we experience victory.

But here's what gets me—even Jesus, the Son of God, right now, in all of His glory is at the right hand of the Father... *waiting* (Hebrews 10:13, ESV)!

Come on now, if Jesus, after everything He went through, is *still waiting* for His enemies to be put under His feet, then we should not complain that we still have to wait!

This heart posture is how you inherit promises: *HE SAT DOWN, WAITING.* Jesus is not frantically pacing heaven trying to get anything to happen outside of the Father's timeline. He is perfectly patient as He waits.

When you are able to go about the process of preparing for your match with the heart posture of being *seated* (not striving or toiling or trying to bring it to pass) and *waiting with patience* (not offended or frustrated at God or living like your life is pointless now)—you will inherit the promise!

You must learn to wait with patience and not be offended at God for taking so long. In other words, it's not a matter of trying to muster up enough faith. Real trust will allow us to endure and wait patiently.

When you wait with patience you will live with purpose.

Seated With Christ

> *And God raised us up with Christ and **seated us with Him** in the heavenly realms in Christ Jesus*
> **Ephesians 2:6**

Here is the great news. The Bible declares that we are *already seated* with Christ. The question is whether or not we will let that heavenly reality work itself out on earth.

Being seated is part of the victory of the cross. You don't have to earn it or work it up. You can only receive it.

When you begin to see yourself as *seated with Jesus right now* in heavenly places, you will welcome that reality here on earth.

Your life will begin to have a supernatural peace as you believe that God has everything under control. All He is asking you to do is *stay seated.*

So don't get up.

Don't let any noises or whispers from the enemy make you jump up and start trying to figure everything out. Rest in God, and trust Him with your future. He has not only died for your sins but welcomed you to sit with Him in victory. Follow His example. Stay seated while you wait.

My Story

During my season of preparation for my perfect match, I was walking in the woods on a summer day with a buddy of mine when a magnificent tree which seemed to stand all alone caught my eye.

Suddenly a strong thought entered my mind, "You are going to propose by that tree." I don't know how to explain this to you other than it was like a thought that wouldn't go away. So I finally said, "Okay, LORD, I believe You!" Then, another thought entered my head, "Promise me that you will." So I told the LORD I would.

After that encounter, I was challenged by the idea that God wants us to have *active* faith, not *passive* faith. He wants us to do things in line with what we believe He is saying.

So while I was single, I wrote a letter to my future wife—asking her to marry me. Then, I had a couple of friends help me bury it one night by that tree and pray over that spot. It was a very special moment. Suffice it to say, I didn't take that moment lightly.

Burying the letter was my simple act of faith—but that was not *all* I was called to do. Even after waiting over three years to break up, taking months off for personal healing, and being very slow about pursuing someone else, I still needed to wait *patiently*.

When I buried that letter, I was walking by faith. But faith isn't the only thing which engages our destiny. It is faith *and* patience.

My point is that when I buried the letter, it would've been great if the next day I was able to go dig it up and propose to my match, but that didn't happen. It wasn't just my *act* of faith—I had to wait patiently, with the right *heart*.

The fact that I had to wait didn't signify a lack on my end. It didn't mean I had messed up or missed the mark. It was simply part of the process.

Patience is waiting with the right heart.

Patience Not Slowness

> *But do not forget this one thing, dear friends: With the Lord a day is like a thousand years, and a thousand years are like a day.* ***The Lord is not slow in keeping his promise,*** *as some understand slowness.* ***Instead He is patient*** *with you...***2 Peter 3:8-9**

This may help put in perspective why the LORD is not worried about speeding things up for you. He is more concerned with bringing you a gift that you are able to maintain than one you have to take back to the store.

If you remember in the Old Testament there were two kings, Saul and David, who illustrated this well. Saul was handed the kingdom in a day and lost it, while David suffered and endured hardships for years. The difference? David *believed* in the promise and *was patient,* and when he finally received the kingdom, *he kept it until the day he died.* It was as if his faith *and patience* allowed him to endure the process of preparation for his destiny so that when he received it, he could maintain it.

It's like how an increasing majority of lottery winners end up bankrupt—they were not fully prepared for how to live with that much money. But the Bible says that whoever gathers little by little will increase it (Proverbs 13:11).

God is not being *slow* about bringing you a perfect match. He is being *patient* toward you. He is waiting until you have all you need to steward what He gives.

Patience is slowness with a purpose.

So don't become discouraged or offended at God that He is making you wait—it is *always* for your good!

Just as this passage suggests, I know that for some of you, one day feels like a thousand years too! But don't forget that there is a purpose in the waiting even when you don't know what that purpose may be. Instead of saying God is slow, start saying that He's patient. Begin shifting your perspective about waiting so that it's in line with His character and purpose.

James 5:7-8 shares an illustration of a farmer waiting for his crop to mature. He knows that being anxious or trying to get the crop to come up quickly won't work. It is futile to try. He also doesn't spend his days looking at the ground.

Farmers don't become fixated on the harvest.

He still has plenty to do and purpose to walk out during growing season before the harvest comes. His every activity during growing season is to *prepare* for harvest. If he tries to pluck up the crop before it has fully matured, it will not be as fruitful as it could've been.

This is the picture of Biblical waiting with the right heart.

The farmer has to wait even though he does not get to see or understand anything that is happening underground. So, be like the farmer who receives a harvest; trust God and wait the right way—with patience!

You will only cause yourself heartache to attempt to harvest the crop too soon.

Purpose In Waiting

"God's geography is not our own. With Him, the shortest distance between any two points may not be a straight line but a meandering trail that seems to lead in the wrong direction or in no direction at all. The delay, common to dreamers, from dream to fulfillment can be absolutely excruciating. No spiritual discipline is as taxing or, for that matter, so close to the heart of holiness as waiting, but that does not mean it is a pleasant experience.

That very season of delay, which we find so distasteful, may, however, be crucial to the plan and purpose of God. Such delays give God time to prepare us for the opportunity and the opportunity for us."

-Excerpt from *Dream*, Mark Rutland[9]

God has a purpose in our waiting, even when we cannot seem to figure out what that purpose may be.

What You Truly Need

*Therefore do not throw away your confidence, which has a great reward. For **you have need of endurance,** so that when you have done the will of God **you may receive what is promised.*** **Hebrews 10:35-36 ESV**

So many times, what we *think* we need is not what we *truly* need. We *think* we need another confirmation from God. We *think* we need God to bring our spouse ASAP. But the Bible says that what we *truly* need is endurance.

In the face of every hardship that comes your way and in spite of every circumstance that seems to go against what God has said to you, *don't give up.*

Maybe you've been doing all of the right things. Perhaps you have been believing God will bring His promise to pass, but you have not seen its fulfillment yet. *Don't give up!*

With the Apostle Paul I would urge you, "Did you suffer so many things in vain—if indeed it was in vain?" (Galatians 3:4, ESV). Has the hardship been simply the *postponement* of deliverance or the *preparation* for it? Have you really gone through everything you've been through for it to all turn out for nothing? No way!

If you have been walking in faith, don't stop now. But make sure you are waiting with the right heart. A heart that endures. A heart that doesn't give up. A heart that is *seated.*

I want to encourage you that it is faith *plus patience* which inherits promises.

So stay seated in Christ, and wait the right way. And then one day you too, like Abraham, *after patiently waiting,* will receive the promise!

11
Perfect Doesn't Mean Easy

Not How I Planned

We grabbed hands and looked at the entrance to the dark woods which lay before us. It was a cold day but starting to get colder as the night took over. I looked at Korie and said, "Once we go in, there's no turning back..."

And off we went. Into the woods and into our destiny.

Neither of us planned to get engaged that soon into our dating relationship, but God intervened in such a powerful way that we had to follow His calling.

Finding the tree was easy, but digging up the letter proved to be a much harder task. It was the start of January, so the ground was not the softest material to work with. Thankfully, it wasn't frozen yet.

All of that would change literally hours later when a huge snow storm covered the ground until Valentine's Day. God called us to dig up the letter at what seemed like the last moment we could've dug it up for some time.

As we shivered in the cold, Korie held a flashlight while I aimlessly dug around the tree. About 30 minutes in, I started to fear that I would never find the letter that I had buried months ago.

I stopped and prayed silently, "God, as best as I know, you called me to do this! So why is this so hard to find?" Instantly I had a sentence pop into my mind the same way God had told me about the tree before: *"Just because I call you to something doesn't mean it is going to be easy."*

That one sentence aptly summarizes what I want you to know before you find your perfect match.

Perfect doesn't mean easy.

Our Perfect Match

After I heard that message from God, it couldn't have been more than a few minutes before I found the letter. In one of the most powerful moments of our lives, I got down on one knee in the middle of the cold dark woods and asked Korie to marry me. And she said yes!

Oh and by the way, for those of you who scoffed at the no-kissing-til-engaged thing, we totally kissed right after she said yes! It was such a perfect moment.

But I have found that it is not the perfect moments that define us. Usually, the hard times shape us and grow us the most. I can say with absolute certainty that our perfect match has been one of the most life-changing, shaping, and sanctifying things in my life.

I have discovered more insecurities and broken places in my life through my relationship with Korie than any other human relationship. Marriage has been a crucible of sanctification for me. And that is a wonderful thing.

There have been many hard times. But they have brought about such a sweetness in my life, our marriage, and my relationship with the LORD which I would not trade for anything!

Many people talk about the "honeymoon phase" in a marriage. They suggest that the first year is amazing and then it gets harder and harder after that. Ours has been the opposite experience.

I am not overstating things to say that our engagement and first year of marriage were *incredibly* difficult! But things have gotten better and better as our marriage has progressed. We truly feel that we are in the best place we have ever been in our relationship, but that has not come without *hard times* of great growth in our lives.

Standing On What God Has Shown You

When hard times come in life, our tendency can be to cut and run. So when hard times come *in a relationship*, the emotional highs of the early days are not enough to sustain us. We need a firmer foundation.

I cannot tell you how many arguments Korie and I had—especially once we got engaged. There's something about knowing you are about to commit the rest of your life to a person that can bring out the worst in you. It's like all of your fears about the future manifest and suddenly, the things that never bothered you become huge issues.

That is why it's so important to seek the LORD about your match *before* you get married. It's imperative to have a list of criteria because there will be plenty of things that try to challenge your belief that you were made for each other.

God so clearly led Korie and me to be together that to end things with her, in my mind, would've been disobeying Him.

I can't stress enough how important it is to be discerning *before* you get deeply committed. If you are able to be confident that you are with the right person, then even when there are major disagreements, you'll stay instead of flee.

All of this is to say that we had great insecurities which needed to be worked out! And that's why I've tried to make it clear throughout this book that while perfect *matches* do exist, perfect *people* don't.

There is no such thing as a perfect relationship. And you must keep this perspective if you are going to walk in love.

Don't Be A Fault-Finder

*Above all, love each other deeply, because **love covers** over a multitude of sins.* **1 Peter 4:8**

When our relationship became more serious, I thought it was my job to *uncover* Korie's faults. It felt like it was my responsibility to make sure that she knew the things she needed to work on. I even thought this was the *loving* thing to do. But that's not Biblical!

Biblical love—the kind that keeps a couple together for life—is the kind that *covers over* the other person's faults. It doesn't mean that you don't have candid conversations about issues in your relationship. It has nothing to do with enabling. It simply means that your *focus* is no longer on their faults but on the amazing person that God has made them to be and is shaping them into.

By the way, as I look back, I cannot even remember what "faults" I was trying to uncover. I have such an amazing wife, and I am in awe of the woman that God has made her into. He has done a much better job than I ever could have!

It's Not Your Job

It is not your job to change your significant other. The pursuit of change *first for yourself* will be the best thing to help them. Jesus put these two realities together when he said:

> *Why do you look at the speck of sawdust in your brother's eye and pay no attention to the plank in your own eye? How can you say to your brother, 'Let me take the speck out of your eye,' when all the time* **there is a plank in your own eye? You hypocrite, first take the plank out of your own eye,** *and then you will see clearly to remove the speck from your brother's eye.* **Matthew 7:3-5**

First of all, I hate it when anyone but me touches my eyes. I mean, isn't the thought of someone poking you in the eyeball absolutely repulsive and intrusive? Just as intrusive is when someone takes it upon themselves to poke around at your problems. What makes it even worse is when the person poking is a *hypocrite*—completely unaware of their own issues. So don't be an eye-poking hypocrite!

Be humble and focus on the things God is doing in your *own* heart.

This passage suggests that working on your own issues will help foster beauty in your partner! But change never comes through being a fault-finder.

When we begin judging someone's motives, it's a telltale sign that we have a log in our eyes. We are not able to help someone properly when we are so fixated on their issue yet unaware of our own.

Let me be clear. There are definitely times to correct people, but never before we are willing to humbly ask God to change us first. That's why Jesus says, "*first take the plank out of your own eye, and then you will see clearly to remove the speck from your brother's eye*" (Matthew 7:5).

When my wife and I stopped worrying about the other person's mess and allowed God to clean up our own, it brought incredible freedom to our relationship!

Rough Patches Are Normal

Let me be the first to tell you that arguments, crying, and disappointments are not abnormal but *normal* because we are *not perfect*.

So just because things are hard doesn't mean that person isn't your perfect match. We are *all* in process with God and need His repair in our lives.

Real love will allow others the freedom to stay in process and not demand instant change or perfection.

We share many details in our book, *Forsaking All Others*, where we break down what God taught us through our struggles, arguments, and first years together. Ultimately, we learned a ton and grew the most by being together.

So don't miss out on the message God gave me: Just because He calls you to something (or someone) doesn't mean it will be easy. Just because there are hard times does not in any way mean you have missed the right person!

In fact, if you are meant to be together, there will inevitably be friction at times because real matches are *purifying* not *enabling*.

Never Partner With Fear

> *There is **no fear in love**. But perfect love drives out fear, because fear has to do with punishment. **The one who fears is not made perfect** in love.* **1 John 4:18**

We could talk a lot here about the sad relationships and even marriages I have seen where a wife has to keep her husband happy all of the time or he will blame *her* for all of his woes.

We could talk about how many relationships are not true *partnerships* but simply two people *keeping up appearances.*

We could talk about the men or women that make each other *walk on eggshells* to keep each other happy. Some have even given up talking about certain subjects for fear of angry outbursts!

I could even share a lot personally about how I used to make my wife afraid to mess up. These are all things that need to be touched by God's love.

Recognize that His love *never* tries to motivate you to change through fear!

In fact, God's love does the opposite! His love *casts out* all fear! Praise Him!

Please hear this warning: Never partner with fear to try to get someone to change!

We have already talked about the dangers of manipulation, but I hope you will take this to heart. *Fear won't change anyone.* If you are someone who makes people afraid to mess up, they may perform differently around *you*, but it will only be because they are afraid to make you upset!

> *Human anger does not produce the righteousness that God desires.* **James 1:20**

When someone does something that is against our desires, it can make us upset. This is one of the key moments to not allow anger to settle in our hearts. When it does, we may unknowingly use that anger to make someone afraid of our displeasure. That is how we often partner with fear. We show our displeasure and intimidate someone into submission through fear.

Human anger *never* brings about the righteousness that God desires.

Of course, we are talking about *unrighteous* anger here. The point is that if your partner knows you will explode or shut down when they mess up, it will never truly change them.

Only God can bring about the *real* change that He desires in their life. Leave it to Him! Free yourself from the emotional ups and downs of monitoring someone's performance!

Sharpness, critical attitudes, making someone walk on eggshells, threats, angry outbursts, and ultimatums are roadblocks to genuine change. God's love is the gateway.

So love someone the way God does and "cover over" their faults (1 Peter 4:8).

No Pressure

If I could change one thing about how my marriage started, it would be embracing the truth that we don't have to get everything right. And most importantly, I would free my wife from any pressure to perform.

One of the most amazing qualities of God is that while *He is in control* (as in sovereign over all), *He does not control* (as in violating our free will).

What I mean is that if you read the entire Bible you will see that God never controls people—and He never instructs us to either. In fact, the only *control* He advises us to make full use of is something called "self-control" (Galatians 5:23). The Bible calls this a fruit of the Spirit. This means it is something that He already possesses and grows in you.

The fruit isn't something you force. Just like how fruit grows in nature without evidence of struggle, so too God produces these things in us without us having to strive. The point I am making is that we have not been given the capacity, gifting, or fruit to control anyone *but ourselves*. And even the way that God produces that ability in us isn't by controlling us but by loving us!

Keep in mind that if you pressure someone into "changing," you'll have to keep pressuring them to maintain it. It's a miserable way to live!

But what freedom to hand over your non-existent job of "controller" to God by trusting Him to bring about change in people through His love—not through fear.

You could say that for Korie and I, it was in the context of our perfect match that God has perfected us the most.

Simply put, it's not your job to change your match. You may have to learn the hard way to not create an environment of control in your relationship, but if you choose the way of love —covering over their faults instead of exposing them—you will discover the freedom of allowing the Holy Spirit to do the work that only He can do.

Perfect doesn't mean easy. But I guarantee you, it is so worth it in the end.

12
Worth the Wait

Tears Of Joy

I couldn't stop the tears from flowing.

In the back office of my soon-to-be bride's hometown church, I called people in one by one to visit with privately before the ceremony began. To me, it was a providential moment to never be forgotten. As I summoned them, person after person came in, and I thanked them with all of my heart for their influence in getting me to this day. My best man, Jason (the man who had held me years before as the pain of a breakup was too much to bear), guarded the door so that no one would interrupt the intimate moments I was having with each person.

But the most significant of those moments was when my mother came in. She knew right away what we had to do.

On our knees together, it felt different than I had imagined— almost like it came quicker than I had expected. Perhaps it was the shock that the day had finally arrived, as if somewhere inside of me, I thought this day may never come.

Either way, there we were in that little back office on our knees, side by side, and holding hands. The tears I cried this time were a different kind. No longer the tears of pain and fear, *these were the tears of joy.*

Sowing And Reaping

Those who sow with tears will reap with songs of joy. Those who go out weeping, carrying seed to sow, **will return** *with songs of joy, carrying sheaves with them.* **Psalm 126:5-6**

I was reaping the joy which pain had planted. This was an incredible return on my investment, trading tears for tears and pain for joy.

I reached into my pocket and pulled out a little baggie. With Sharpie marker, I had written the date and time on the outside—as if I could ever forget when and where that ziplock bag of old tissues had come from. Contained in it were the old tears. Dried up now by the days which had passed. But the tears were still speaking, still representing the fact that it was *all* true—*all of it.*

The tears planted long ago cultivated this day of destiny.

I cannot tell you how powerful it was to hold a physical symbol that *God had literally turned my tears into joy.*

If I could only bottle up that feeling and give you a taste... perhaps that has been my attempt in writing this book.

Suddenly Psalm 56:8 had a totally new meaning:

You keep track of all my sorrows. You have collected all my tears in your bottle. You have recorded each one in your book. **Psalm 56:8 NLT**

If I could've known back then that it would all be okay—that God really did have someone for me, I would like to think that I wouldn't have been so afraid of making the wrong decision.

I think I would've relaxed more and fully enjoyed my season of singleness.

If I could've had just one polaroid picture of my wedding day to hold on to a few years prior, I'd like to think that I wouldn't have doubted God.

But then, that wouldn't have been faith, would it?

Faith clings to things which are *unseen* (2 Corinthians 4:18).

Your Choice

My question for you is simple: In light of everything you have read in this book, will you choose to be a person who walks by faith and waits on God to bring your perfect match?

All I can say is that it is worth it—all of the pain, wondering, dryness, longing, brokenness, hardships, and waiting.

Inheriting promises is always worth the wait.

My Perfect Match

There she was all dressed in white
Finally I saw my destiny in sight
She walked down the aisle with incredible grace
And I'll never forget the look on her face

If only I'd known this was how I'd feel
The joy of the moment was so surreal
Never thought it would come this quick
All those nights I was worried sick

The times I thought God had passed over me
Stoked fires of insecurity
But if He would've brought her before I was ready
Our relationship would not have been steady

It wasn't to cause me unneeded pain
Or to make loneliness drive me insane
In the midst of the silence, I finally learned
That a perfect match can never be earned

It's only received as I walk in faith
And with patience, learn how to wait
Until God's plan comes to pass
Though He may not move too fast

I'm so glad I waited and did it His way
So looking back, I won't have to say
That I forced something that wasn't His plan
Or always had to understand

I stopped striving to achieve my goal
And let go of all control
To the One who has the power to make
An effortless match without the heartache

Seeing her come down the aisle I felt
Something inside me begin to melt
These were a different kind of tears
Worth every single one of those years

That I chose to believe there was someone for me
And learned to trust God's sovereignty
I found out that He can always be trusted
Even when my plans seem to be busted

Though I often wanted to quit
God taught me the power of learning to sit
And not just trying to make the time pass
He gave me contentment, a kind that would last

It was worth it all—I'd do it again
In exchange for knowing my very best friend
I would not trade what we have now
For a few less years of waiting around

And though we've had to keep on growing
Hard times together were simply showing
That we had to fight the big temptation
Of making each other our foundation

Instead of delighting in God alone
The most Perfect Match we've ever known
To Him alone belongs the glory
For He's the author of our story

Even through all of those growing years
And countless bottles of my tears
God knew the end from the beginning
I didn't need to keep plates spinning.

I needed to trust His timing was best
That all He wanted from me was to rest
While waiting for His plan to hatch
I finally found my perfect match

May God do the same for you as you delight yourself in Him!

Afterword:
It Can Happen to You

Do you remember my friend Barry who was instrumental in helping me move from complacency to trusting God for His will in my life?

Years later, he called me to his office on campus and asked me to speak to his son, Jacob (not his real name). I didn't have much of a context for what was going on in his life other than he was engaged and uncertain about his future.

We decided to meet at Dairy Queen.

Without telling him what to do, I simply shared my story. I even told him about how his father had been instrumental in teaching me about God-honoring relationships. I told him how ending my relationship was the hardest thing I had ever done but also the most rewarding.

We talked for over three hours.

It felt like God was literally pouring out His wisdom as we spoke. I didn't know what Jacob would do, but I knew he couldn't stay where he was. Something shifted in him that night.

When we parted ways, I called Barry and told him how it went. We prayed for God to lead Jacob clearly and reveal His plan.

In the coming days, Jacob did the hardest thing he had ever done and ended his engagement.

While I don't know all of the details, I do know it was incredibly painful for him and I'm sure even more so for her. Stepping out in faith often exposes the fears and barren places in our souls—bringing them to the surface for the Healer to repair.

I saw Jacob several more times over the next few years. Each time he seemed more secure, content, and convinced that God was working behind the scenes to bring his perfect match.

She didn't come right way.

Although Jacob acted in *faith*, that wasn't the only necessary ingredient—he also had to have *patience*. And in the quietness of singleness, he was prepared and strengthened by God.

I've got to be honest; I was super impressed with how well he waited. God had graciously allowed me to get married about a year and a half after I went through my painful breakup. Jacob waited longer. But I never saw him act out of insecurity or pursue wrong relationships.

One day, I got a phone call from Jacob excitedly wanting to meet up. He asked if he could bring a "friend."

From the moment I met Sarah (not her real name), I could tell he had found the one. I had never seen him so happy or alive. And although they had to learn and grow through their own share of hardship, Jacob finally found his perfect match.

He had faith, learned patience, and inherited promises. And the same God who did it for him and for me is willing to do it for you too. He is not a respecter of persons (Romans 2:11), and He is the same yesterday, today, and forever (Hebrews 13:8).

That includes your history and your destiny!

> ***Now to Him who is able*** *to do immeasurably more than all we ask or imagine, according to His power that is at work within us, to Him be glory in the church and in Christ Jesus throughout all generations, for ever and ever! Amen.* **Ephesians 3:20-21**

God is able! It happened to me. It happened to Jacob. And it can happen to you.

So walk in faith, be patient, and trust God to fulfill your destiny and bring along your perfect match!

Notes

1) "Strong's Hebrew: 2896a. Tob -- Pleasant, Agreeable, Good." http://biblehub.com/hebrew/2896a.htm.

2) "Strong's Hebrew: 3966. מְאֹד (meod) -- Muchness, Force, Abundance." http://biblehub.com/hebrew/3966.htm.

3) "Strong's Greek: 5550. χρόνος (chronos) -- Time." http://biblehub.com/greek/5550.htm.

4) Courson, Jon. "Seachlight with Jon Courson." Searchlight with Pastor Jon Courson. https://www.joncourson.com/.

5) Vallotton, Kris. Heavy Rain: How to Flood Your World with God's Transforming Power. Minneapolis, MN: Chosen, 2016.

6) Coy, Bob. One Surrendered Life: A Testimony of the Power of God Displayed in the Life of an Ordinary Man. Fort Lauderdale, FL: Calvary Chapel Church Fort Lauderdale, 2005.

7) Stanley, Andy. "The New Rules for Love, Sex & Dating." North Point. http://northpoint.org/messages/the-new-rules-for-love-sex-and-dating.

8) Cowman, Lettie Burd, and James Reimann. *Streams in the Desert*. Grand Rapids, MI: Zondervan, 1997.

9) Rutland, Mark. *Dream*. Lake Mary, FL: Charisma House, 2003.

Appendix:
Who Are You?

One of the most important questions that was asked in the book was: *"Who is (you) if you're not with a man or woman?"*

It is interesting to me how *being with* another person has the ability to shape who we *think* we are.

And *being without* another person also has that power.

But the Bible teaches that the *only person* who has the power to *change your identity* is Jesus Christ. In other words, if you're *with Him*, you'll know who you are. You become a child of God. *He* becomes your identity, and you will never again need the approval of another person for fulfillment.

The cure for co-dependency is actually total dependency—on Jesus.

The crisis of our day is a culture filled with people who do not know who they really are. I know from experience that not being grounded as a son or daughter of God produces a roller-coaster existence.

> *That we may no longer be children, **tossed to and fro by the waves.*** **Ephesians 4:14 ESV**

Does your life ever feel this way—*tossed to and fro by the waves?*

I have good news for you. It doesn't have to!

God has created the provision we need to become His sons and daughters by sending His Son Jesus to die on the cross for us.

Now please hear me out. I have met *many* people who never realized that the Bible says we must *accept* Jesus to be saved from our sins and become God's children.

> Yet to all who did **receive Him**, to those who **believed in His name**, He gave the right to become children of God. **John 1:12**

To become children of God, we simply need to *receive* Jesus. The above verse shows us that "receiving Jesus" actually means "believing in His name." Simply put, this means accepting Him entirely, including all that He has done for us.

I have interacted with hundreds of college students and adults alike who thought that going to church meant they had a relationship with God. They were under the impression that church attendance would get them into heaven when they died.

But the Bible is clear:

> If you **declare with your mouth,** "Jesus is Lord," **and believe in your heart** that God raised Him from the dead, you will be saved. **Romans 10:9**

Have you made this decision? Have you made this confession and believed in your heart that Jesus died, was buried, and was raised for *you?*

He did all of this to pay for your sins and bring you into a son or daughter relationship with God!

> *Suppose one of you has a hundred sheep and loses one of them.* ***Doesn't he leave the ninety-nine*** *in the open country* ***and go after the lost sheep*** *until he finds it?* **Luke 15:4**

It may be easy to believe that God loves the world or died for *other* people's sins; but the Bible teaches that He did it for *you*. He left the ninety-nine to come after the one. And guess what? *You are the one!* The focus isn't on what He has done for everyone else but for *you*.

If you have never invited Jesus into your heart by repenting of your sins and believing that He paid for them on the cross, would you pray this prayer right now?

> *Dear God,*
>
> *I confess to you that I have not lived the way You desire. I have sinned against You, and for that I am truly sorry. I am making a decision today to once and for all place my faith in what Jesus has done for me. I want to be Your son/daughter. Please forgive me of all of my sins. I confess that Jesus died, was buried, and rose from the dead* ***for me***. *I invite you today to be my Savior, my Lord, my Father, and my Friend.*
>
> *In Jesus' Name,*
>
> *Amen*

If you sincerely prayed that prayer, I believe that God—who cannot lie (Titus 1:2)—has been faithful to His Word, and you have become His child! Congratulations! This is the best and most life-changing decision you could ever make.

My suggestion to you is to get into a good Bible-teaching church and grow in your relationship with the LORD. May you become a person who is so grounded in your identity with God that you are "no longer tossed to and fro by the waves" (Ephesians 4:14, ESV).

God bless you!

Wes Raley

About the Author:

Wes and his wife Korie live in Indiana and have four young children: Isaac, Grace, Luke, and Valorie. After many years of waiting, they finally found each other and are happily enjoying God's perfect match. They continue to coach singles and couples from the wisdom of God's Word and the lessons learned through their times of singleness, dating, engagement, and marriage. Openly sharing their struggles and breakthroughs has helped many people walk in healthy, fulfilling, God-centered relationships.

Are you ready to find the one?

For relationship tools for singles including the "Finding the One" E-Course and personal coaching with Wes and Korie, visit:

www.perfectmatchcoaching.com

HALF OFF COUPON

50% OFF

FINDING THE ONE E-COURSE AT

perfectmatchcoaching.com

50% OFF

USE CODE: READERBONUS

Coming Soon:

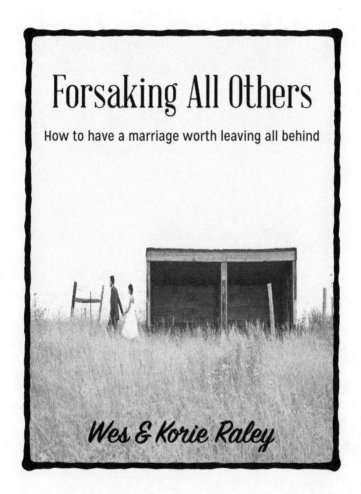

Forsaking All Others

How to have a marriage worth leaving all behind

Wes & Korie Raley

Visit:
www.forsakingallothersbook.com

CPSIA information can be obtained
at www.ICGtesting.com
Printed in the USA
BVHW032119010419
544332BV00001B/69/P